STATE
THE
STATE

More Than 2,500 Questions and Answers from
Alabama to **Wyoming**

Every Answer is a State!

by

Gilbert W. Davies

HiStory ink Books
P.O. BOX 52
HAT CREEK, CA 96040

Other HiStory ink Books:

STORIES OF THE KLAMATH NATIONAL FOREST—THE FIRST 50 YEARS: 1905 – 1955

MEMORIES FROM THE LAND OF SISKIYOU: PAST LIVES AND TIMES IN SISKIYOU COUNTY

FORT JONES (CA) 1852 – 1858: MILITARY NOTES

A WORLD WAR II DIARY BY LAWRENCE E. DAVIES, THE WEST COAST CORRESPONDENT FOR THE NEW YORK TIMES

PHOTOGRAPHIC IMAGES OF THE KLAMATH NATIONAL FOREST IN SISKIYOU AND HUMBOLDT COUNTIES: A HISTORICAL JOURNEY

HISTORICAL AND COMMEMORATIVE SIGNS, PLAQUES AND MONUMENTS IN SISKIYOU COUNTY, CALIFORNIA

THIRTY COUNTRY ROAD LOOP TRIPS IN NORTHERN CALIFORNIA: ALL NORTH OF SACRAMENTO

© 1994 by Gilbert W. Davies
Library of Congress Catalog Card Number: 94-75126
ISBN 0-9634413-4-5
Printed by CAT Publishing Company, P.O. Box 992197, Redding, CA 96099-2197

CONTENTS

FORWARD

There are only fifty possible answers to the more than 2,500 questions and match-ups. Every answer is the name of a state. Even if you don't know the answer you have at least a one in fifty chance of being right. For most of the multiple choice or matching questions you have a better than one in fifty chance since the states involved are listed in alphabetical order with the question. Only those states listed are to be used for an answer to a particular question.

This is a book for individuals or groups. There are no trick questions. You may want to refer to a map of the United States after answering questions on shapes, boundaries, highways, trails, locations, distances or directions.

So have fun while making your statement. Remember: *Nothing stated – nothing gained*.

BORDERS AND BOUNDARIES

1. Which has the longer coastline: Alaska or the total forty-eight contiguous states?

2. Parts of the northern boundaries of which states run along the 49th parallel north (divides Canada with U. S.)?

3. Lake Michigan bounds or is part of which four states?

4. Which has the longer coastline—Florida or Hawaii?

5. Which two states do not border any other states?

6. Name the ten states that border the Mississippi River.

7. Chihuahua, a Mexican state, has a common boundary with what two states?

8. Sonora, a Mexican state, has a common boundary with what two states?

9. The boundary between which two states forms an arc?

10. Which two states share Lake Tahoe?

11. Lake Champlain partially divides what two states?

12. What are the only two states that adjoin seven other states?

13. There is only one point in the United States common to four states. Name the states.

14. The Cumberland Gap is in the vicinity of what three states?

15. The Province of Quebec has a common border with what four states?

16. Waterton National Park in Canada borders what state?

17. Saskatchewan has a common border with what two states?

18. Manitoba has a common border with what two states?

19. From what state can one go south into every one of the six states bordering it?

20. What five states does the Gulf of Mexico border?

21. What state has the shortest coastline?

22. What two states are bordered by eight others?

23. What state is bounded by only one other state?

24. Lake Erie bounds or is part of what four states?

25. Quetico Provincial Park in Canada is across the border from what state?

26. The Mexican town of Ciudad Juarez is across the border from what state?

27. The slogan "54-40 or fight," referred to the proposed boundary between Canada and what United States territory?

28. What state has the second longest coastline and shoreline?

29. The Mason-Dixon Line became part of the boundary between what states?

30. What five states are considered the "border states" (Slave states adjacent to the free states)?

31. Two of the three states share a common border. Name the one that doesn't touch either of the others.

    a. Oklahoma, Missouri, Louisiana
    b. Kansas, Iowa, South Dakota
    c. Kentucky, North Carolina, Ohio
    d. Florida, Alabama, South Carolina
    e. Washington, Montana, North Dakota
    f. Nevada, Colorado, Idaho
    g. Michigan, Wisconsin, Nebraska
    h. Maine, Vermont, Massachusetts
    i. Pennsylvania, Virginia, Delaware
    j. Tennessee, Mississippi, West Virginia

32. Portions of state boundaries are often determined by a river. Name the missing state.

    a. The Ohio River divides Indiana and _____
    b. The Missouri River divides Iowa and _____
    c. The Mississippi River divides Minnesota and _____
    d. The Colorado River divides California and _____
    e. The Rio Grande River divides Coahuila and _____
    f. The Savannah River divides Georgia and _____
    g. The Connecticut River divides Vermont and _____
    h. The Snake River divides Oregon and _____
    i. The Red River divides Oklahoma and _____

ANSWERS TO
BORDERS AND BOUNDARIES

1. Alaska

2. Washington, Idaho, Montana, North Dakota, Minnesota

3. Illinois, Indiana, Michigan, Wisconsin

4. Florida

5. Alaska and Hawaii

6. Arkansas, Illinois, Iowa, Kentucky, Louisiana, Minnesota, Mississippi, Missouri, Tennessee, Wisconsin

7. Texas and New Mexico

8. New Mexico and Arizona

9. Pennsylvania and Delaware

10. California and Nevada

11. New York and Vermont

12. Colorado and Kentucky

13. Arizona, Colorado, New Mexico, Utah

14. Kentucky, Tennessee, Virginia

15. Maine, New Hampshire, New York, Vermont

16. Montana

17. Montana and North Dakota

18. Minnesota and North Dakota

19. Arkansas

20. Alabama, Florida, Louisiana, Mississippi, Texas

21. New Hampshire

22. Missouri and Tennessee

23. Maine

24. Michigan, New York, Ohio, Pennsylvania

25. Minnesota

26. Texas

27. Oregon

28. Florida

29. Pennsylvania–Maryland and Pennsylvania–Virginia

30. Delaware, Kentucky, Maryland, Missouri, Virginia

31. a. Louisiana
    b. Kansas
    c. North Carolina
    d. South Carolina
    e. Washington
    f. Colorado
    g. Nebraska
    h. Maine
    i. Virginia
    j. West Virginia

32. a. Kentucky
    b. Nebraska
    c. Wisconsin
    d. Arizona
    e. Texas
    f. South Carolina
    g. New Hampshire
    h. Idaho
    i. Texas

CITIES, COUNTIES, CAPITALS AND CAPITOLS

1. In which state is the tallest state capitol building?

2. What state capitol building has the largest wooden dome in the country?

3. What state capitol building is decorated with volcanic rock on the outside?

4. What state capitol building has a rotunda and dome copied from Napoleon's tomb in Paris?

5. What state capitol building has a main dome surrounded by four smaller domes?

6. What state capitol building has an oil well on the grounds?

7. What state capitol building has the only capitol dome made of granite?

8. What state capitol building was designed by Thomas Jefferson?

9. What state capitol is an 18-story-tall building?

10. What state capitol building is built in the shape of an Indian Zia (sun) symbol?

11. What state capitol building was shelled during the Civil War?

12. What state capitol building is the oldest statehouse in which the legislature still meets?

13. What state capitol building is topped by a 120-foot-high cupola?

14. What state capitol building is made of marble from every marble producing country in the world?

15. What state capitol building is built of 25 kinds of marble, limestone, sandstone and granite?

16. What state capitol building was built in 1792 and is one of the oldest statehouses still in use?

17. What state capitol building has the second largest, freestanding marble dome in the world (second in size to that of St. Peter's Basilica in Rome)?

18. Four state capitals have the word "City" in the name. Name them.

19. In which state has the capital been changed fifteen times?

20. Which state has divisions instead of counties?

21. Which state has parishes instead of counties?

22. Which state east of the Mississippi River has the most counties?

23. Which state has the least number of counties?

24. In what state is Bourbon County?

25. What four states start with the same letter as the names of their capitals?

26. What state has the most counties?

27. Which two states have had two capitals at the same time?

28. a. Which state has the only county touching four other states?
    b. Name the four states the county touches?

29. The oldest incorporated city in the United States is in what state?

30. In which states are the highest and lowest (elevation) incorporated cities in the United States?

31. The oldest town of European origin in the United States is in what state?

32. This capital city is considered to be the oldest in any state. Name the state?

33. In which state was the second capital of the Confederate States?

34. Which state has the capital located at the junction of the Grand and Red Cedar rivers?

35. What state has the capital located along the Susquehanna River?

36. Which two state have capitals located along the Mississippi River?

37. What state had it's capital settled by squatters?

38. In what state was the current capital originally named Providence?

39. Of the forty-eight contiguous states, which have the southernmost, northernmost and westernmost capitals?

40. The name of the state capital of which state means "red stick" in French?

41. In what state was the first capital of the Confederate States?

42. Which state has the capital that receives the highest average annual snowfall?

43. What two states have capitals that the 45th parallel passes through (halfway between the equator and the North Pole)?

44. The windiest capital is in which state?

45. Which state capital was laid out in the form of a Maltese cross—eight miles north to south and seven miles east to west?

46. In what state does the name of the capital rhyme with the word "cheer?"

47. Two historic mining towns are named Virginia City. In which two states are they located?

48. In which state is the smallest county in the United States (not counting Virginia which has independent cities with the status of counties)?

49. In what state do more than 35 cities have independent status similar to a county?

50. Times Square is in what state?

51. Which state has a capital named after a President?

52. In what state is the city known as the "Pittsburgh of the South?"

53. In which state is the capital called "City of Roses?"

54. The highest state capital in elevation is in which state?

55. Only one state capital starts with each of the following letters: F, I, N. Which three states are they in?

56. Springfield is a name common to many states. In which states are the four largest cities with the name Springfield?

57. Thirteen states each have a Washington, Jefferson and Lincoln county. Name as many as you can.

58. Mississippi County is located in two states. Name them.

59. Texas County is located in two states. Name them.

60. Iowa County is located in two states. Name them.

61. Coos County is located in two states. Name them.

62. Ohio County is located in three states. Name at least two of them.

63. Wyoming County is located in three states. Name at least two of them.

64. Potter County is located in three states. Name at least two of them.

65. Fremont County is located in four states. Name at least three of them.

66. Delaware County is located in six states. Name at least four of them.

67. Custer County is located in six states. Name at least four of them.

68. Orange County is located in eight states. Name at least five of them.

69. Two state capitals begin and end with the same letter in their name. What are the states they are in?

70. Nine state capitals have two or more words in their name. Name the states they are in.

71. In what state is the town of Truth or Consequences?

72. The towns of Ajo and Why are located near each other in what state?

73. The towns of Igo and Ono are located near each other in what state?

74. The villages of Trickem and Skinnem are in what state?

75. In what state are the villages of Grasshopper and Bumble Bee?

76. In what state are the villages of Difficult and Defeated?

77. In what state may be found the following towns: New Boston, New Concord, New Lexington, New Plymouth, New Philadelphia?

78. The following villages or towns are all found in what state: George, Ira, Luther, Malcom, Rodney?

79. The following villages or towns are all found in what state: Ella, Inez, Lola, Mary Alice, Minnie, Phyllis?

80. The towns of Home Place, Melody Hill and Harmony are all found in what state?

81. The towns of Blessing, Comfort, Happy and Humble are all found in what state?

82. The towns of Christiansburg, Churchtown and Assumption are all found in what state?

83. The towns of Christmas, Homeland and Holiday are all found in what state?

84. The towns of Nissequogue, Ronkonkoma and Skaneateles are all found in what state?

85. In the following 20 parts, match the names of the settlement, hamlet, village, town or city to the states they are in as listed. Use only those states listed.

    Part I: a. Promised Land   (1) New Mexico
                        b. Angel Fire   (2) South Carolina
                        c. Burning Bush   (3) Texas

Part II: a. Soldier (1) Colorado
 b. Rifle (2) Illinois
 c. Marine (3) Kentucky

Part III: a. Fossil (1) Colorado
 b. Dinosaur (2) Iowa
 c. Ages (3) Kentucky
 d. Olds (4) Oregon

Part IV: a. Mars (1) Florida
 b. Jupiter (2) Florida
 c. Neptune (3) New Jersey
 d. Venus (4) Pennsylvania

Part V: a. Cuba (1) Alabama
 b. Canada (2) Florida
 c. Switzerland (3) Indiana
 d. China (4) Kentucky

Part VI: a. Fourmile (1) Indiana
 b. Seven Mile (2) Kentucky
 c. Tenmile (3) Ohio
 d. Twelve Mile (4) Oregon

Part VII: a. Sun (1) Louisiana
 b. Sunrise (2) New York
 c. Sundance (3) Texas
 d. Sunset (4) Wyoming

Part VIII: a. Tippecanoe (1) Indiana
 b. Tippi (2) Kentucky
 c. Canoe (3) Mississippi
 d. Tyler (4) Texas

Part IX: a. Canaan (1) Connecticut
 b. Bethlehem (2) Idaho
 c. Eden (3) Kentucky
 d. Nazareth (4) Pennsylvania

Part X: a. Soso (1) California
 b. Toast (2) Massachusetts
 c. Rough and Ready (3) Mississippi
 d. Luck (4) North Carolina
 e. Sandwich (5) Wisconsin

Part XI:	a. Big Bug	(1) Arizona
	b. Bug Hill	(2) Arkansas
	c. Black Gnat	(3) Colorado
	d. Bugscuffle	(4) Kentucky
	e. Yellow Jacket	(5) North Carolina
Part XII:	a. Nevada	(1) Colorado
	b. Alabama	(2) Iowa
	c. Oregon	(3) Minnesota
	d. Wyoming	(4) Missouri
	e. Texas	(5) New York
Part XIII:	a. Paris	(1) Arizona
	b. Cairo	(2) Arkansas
	c. London	(3) Idaho
	d. Bagdad	(4) Nebraska
	e. Florence	(5) Oregon
Part XIV:	a. Pulse	(1) Idaho
	b. Bone	(2) Indiana
	c. Cataract	(3) Kentucky
	d. Dimple	(4) Michigan
	e. Colon	(5) Ohio
Part XV:	a. Cucumber	(1) Indiana
	b. Plum	(2) Michigan
	c. Pimento	(3) Pennsylvania
	d. Turkey	(4) Texas
	e. Jam	(5) West Virginia
Part XVI:	a. Tea	(1) Florida
	b. Sassafras	(2) Kentucky
	c. Filbert	(3) Pennsylvania
	d. Fries	(4) South Dakota
	e. Spuds	(5) Virginia
Part XVII:	a. Leakesville	(1) Colorado
	b. Spillville	(2) Iowa
	c. Crain	(3) Kentucky
	d. Wetmore	(4) Mississippi
	e. Quicksand	(5) Oregon

Part XVIII:
a. Oconomowoc
b. Assinippi
c. Loogootee
d. Mattawamkeag
e. Lukachukai
f. Wachapreague

(1) Arizona
(2) Illinois
(3) Maine
(4) Massachusetts
(5) Virginia
(6) Wisconsin

Part XIX:
a. Zero
b. Seventeen
c. Forty Four
d. Eighty Four
e. Eighty Eight
f. Ninety Six
g. Hundred

(1) Arkansas
(2) Kentucky
(3) Montana
(4) Ohio
(5) Pennsylvania
(6) South Carolina
(7) West Virginia

Part XX:
a. Coronado
b. Marquette
c. Cortez
d. Ponce de Leon
e. Joliet
f. De Soto
g. Cadillac

(1) California
(2) Colorado
(3) Florida
(4) Illinois
(5) Michigan
(6) Mississippi
(7) Wisconsin

86. Match the ghost town to the states listed.

Part I:
a. Skidoo
b. Belmont
c. Mercur
d. Carbon
e. Crystal
f. Cornucopia

(1) California
(2) Colorado
(3) Nevada
(4) Oregon
(5) Utah
(6) Wyoming

Part II:
a. Bay Horse
b. Old Toroda
c. Iditarod
d. Cabezon
e. Signal
f. Carbonate

(1) Alaska
(2) Arizona
(3) Idaho
(4) New Mexico
(5) South Dakota
(6) Washington

87. Name the state that does not include the designated town or city.

Part I:

a. Salem .... Oregon, New Jersey, Massachusetts, Tennessee

b. Anderson .... Indiana, Texas, Illinois, South Carolina

c. Portland .... New Jersey, Maine, Oregon, Indiana

d. Columbus .... Ohio, Missouri, Mississippi, Georgia

e. Richmond ...... West Virginia, California, Virginia, Kentucky

f. Lancaster .... Pennsylvania, Ohio, California, North Carolina

g. Chester .... North Dakota, South Carolina, Pennsylvania, Montana

h. Madison .... Iowa, Wisconsin, South Dakota, Indiana

i. Nashville .... Kentucky, Tennessee, Arkansas, Georgia

j. Jackson .... Michigan, Mississippi, Missouri, Maryland

Part II:

a. Jacksonville ... Texas, Oklahoma, Florida, Illinois

b. York .... Pennsylvania, Rhode Island, Maine, Nebraska

c. Newark .... New Jersey, Virginia, Delaware, Ohio

d. Akron .... Colorado, Ohio, New York, Vermont

e. Albany .... Iowa, New York, Missouri, Kentucky

f. Lincoln .... Nebraska, California, Illinois, Texas

g. Hudson .... Michigan, New York, Wisconsin, Vermont

h. Manchester ... Iowa, Kentucky, Rhode Island, New Hampshire

i. Montgomery .. Virginia, West Virginia, Alabama, Minnesota

j. Columbia .... Tennessee, South Carolina, Massachusetts, Pennsylvania

88. Match the nicknames of the cities to the states listed.

   Part I:

   a. Big Apple
   b. Convention City
   c. Cereal City
   d. Windy City
   e. Big D
   f. Derby City
   g. Crescent City
   h. Biggest Little City in the World
   i. Mission City
   j. Glass Capital of the World

   (1) Illinois
   (2) Kentucky
   (3) Louisiana
   (4) Michigan
   (5) Nevada
   (6) New Jersey
   (7) New York
   (8) Ohio
   (9) Texas
   (10) Texas

   Part II:

   a. Financial Capital of the South
   b. Pittsburgh of the South
   c. Queen City of the Lakes
   d. Porkopolis
   e. Mile-High City
   f. Motor City
   g. Steel Town
   h. Insurance City
   i. Gateway to the West
   j. Oil Capital of the World

   (1) Alabama
   (2) Colorado
   (3) Connecticut
   (4) Georgia
   (5) Indiana
   (6) Michigan
   (7) Missouri
   (8) New York
   (9) Ohio
   (10) Oklahoma

89. In what states are the following towns and cities? Each state is represented once in this 50 part question. Although some names may be in more than one state, the town or city with the largest population is the right one. Use only those states listed in each part.

   Part I:

   a. New Castle
   b. Tempe
   c. Hilo
   d. Sarasota
   e. Redding
   f. Warm Springs
   g. Golden
   h. Eureka Springs
   i. Kodiak
   j. Groton

   (1) Alaska
   (2) Arizona
   (3) Arkansas
   (4) California
   (5) Colorado
   (6) Connecticut
   (7) Delaware
   (8) Florida
   (9) Georgia
   (10) Hawaii

Part II:

a. New Harmony	(1) Idaho
b. Bangor	(2) Illinois
c. Bowling Green	(3) Indiana
d. Coeur d'Alene	(4) Iowa
e. Hyannis	(5) Kansas
f. Nauvoo	(6) Kentucky
g. New Iberia	(7) Louisiana
h. Council Bluffs	(8) Maine
i. St. Mary's City	(9) Maryland
j. Dodge City	(10) Massachusetts

Part III:

a. Grand Island	(1) Michigan
b. Hanover	(2) Minnesota
c. Bemidji	(3) Mississippi
d. Butte	(4) Missouri
e. Los Alamos	(5) Montana
f. Battle Creek	(6) Nebraska
g. Elko	(7) Nevada
h. St. Joseph	(8) New Hampshire
i. Wildwood	(9) New Jersey
j. Oxford	(10) New Mexico

Part IV:

a. Pendleton	(1) New York
b. Lead	(2) North Carolina
c. Erie	(3) North Dakota
d. Tarrytown	(4) Ohio
e. Clemson	(5) Oklahoma
f. Bartlesville	(6) Oregon
g. Fargo	(7) Pennsylvania
h. Marietta	(8) Rhode Island
i. Narragansett	(9) South Carolina
j. Winston-Salem	(10) South Dakota

Part V:

a. Green Bay	(1) Alabama
b. Sheridan	(2) Tennessee
c. Anacortes	(3) Texas
d. Gatlinburg	(4) Utah
e. Williamsburg	(5) Vermont
f. Tuskegee	(6) Virginia
g. Corpus Christi	(7) Washington
h. Morgantown	(8) West Virginia
i. Moab	(9) Wisconsin
j. Barre	(10) Wyoming

ANSWERS TO
CITIES, COUNTIES, CAPITALS AND CAPITOLS

1. Louisiana (450-feet-high)

2. Maryland

3. Hawaii

4. Kentucky

5. Iowa

6. Oklahoma

7. Wisconsin

8. Virginia

9. North Dakota

10. New Mexico

11. South Carolina

12. New Hampshire

13. Nevada

14. Louisiana

15. Minnesota

16. Delaware

17. Rhode Island

18. Missouri (Jefferson City), Nevada (Carson City), Oklahoma (Oklahoma City), Utah (Salt Lake City)

19. Texas

20. Alaska

21. Louisiana

22. Georgia (159)

23. Delaware (3)

24. Kentucky

25. Delaware (Dover), Hawaii (Honolulu), Indiana (Indianapolis), Oklahoma (Oklahoma City)

26. Texas (254)

27. Rhode Island (Newport and Providence), Connecticut (Hartford & New Haven)

28. a. Oklahoma (Cimarron County)
    b. Colorado, Kansas, New Mexico, Texas

29. Maine (York – incorporated under the name Georgiana in 1642)

30. Colorado (Leadville – 10,152 feet), California (Calipatria – 184 feet below sea level)

31. Florida (St. Augustine – founded in 1565)

32. New Mexico (Santa Fe – 1609)

33. Virginia (Richmond)

34. Michigan (Lansing)

35. Pennsylvania (Harrisburg)

36. Minnesota (St. Paul), Louisiana (Baton Rouge)

37. Wyoming (Cheyenne – 1867)

38. Maryland (Annapolis – founded as Providence in 1649)

39. Texas (Austin – southernmost), Washington (Olympia – northernmost), Oregon (Salem – westernmost)

40. Louisiana (Baton Rouge)

41. Alabama (Montgomery)

42. Alaska (Juneau – receives an average of 100 inches of snow annually)

43. Oregon (Salem) and Minnesota (St. Paul)

44. Wyoming (Cheyenne – wind blows an average of 13 miles per hour)

45. Ohio (Columbus)

46. South Dakota (Pierre)

47. Montana and Nevada

48. Rhode Island (Bristol County – 24 square miles)

49. Virginia

50. New York

51. Nebraska (Lincoln)

52. Alabama (Birmingham)

53. Arkansas (Little Rock)

54. New Mexico (Santa Fe)

55. Kentucky (Frankfort), Indiana (Indianapolis), Tennessee (Nashville)

56. Illinois, Massachusetts, Missouri, Ohio

57. Arkansas, Colorado, Georgia, Idaho, Kansas, Kentucky, Mississippi, Missouri, Nebraska, Oklahoma, Oregon, Tennessee, Wisconsin (Louisiana has parishes with all three names)

58. Arkansas and Missouri

59. Missouri and Oklahoma

60. Iowa and Wisconsin

61. New Hampshire and Oregon

62. Indiana, Kentucky, West Virginia

63. New York, Pennsylvania, West Virginia

64. Pennsylvania, South Dakota, Texas

65. Colorado, Idaho, Iowa, Wyoming

66. Indiana, Iowa, New York, Ohio, Oklahoma, Pennsylvania

67. Colorado, Idaho, Montana, Nebraska, Oklahoma, South Dakota

68. California, Florida, Indiana, New York, North Carolina, Texas, Vermont, Virginia

69. Georgia (Atlanta), Maine (Augusta)

70. Arkansas (Little Rock), Iowa (Des Moines), Louisiana (Baton Rouge), Missouri (Jefferson City), Minnesota (St. Paul), Nevada (Carson City), New Mexico (Santa Fe), Oklahoma (Oklahoma City), Utah (Salt Lake City)

71. New Mexico

72. Arizona

73. California

74. Alabama

75. Arizona

76. Tennessee

77. Ohio

78. Iowa

79. Kentucky

80. Indiana

81. Texas

82. Ohio

83. Florida

84. New York

85. Part I: a. (2) South Carolina
                 b. (1) New Mexico
                 c. (3) Texas

     Part II: a. (3) Kentucky
                 b. (1) Colorado
                 c. (2) Illinois

Part III:	a.	(4)	Oregon	Part XIII:	a.	(3) Idaho
	b.	(1)	Colorado		b.	(4) Nebraska
	c.	(3)	Kentucky		c.	(2) Arkansas
	d.	(2)	Iowa		d.	(1) Arizona
					e.	(5) Oregon
Part IV:	a.	(4)	Pennsylvania			
	b.	(1)	Florida	Part XIV:	a.	(5) Ohio
	c.	(3)	New Jersey		b.	(1) Idaho
	d.	(2)	Florida		c.	(2) Indiana
					d.	(3) Kentucky
Part V:	a.	(1)	Alabama		e.	(4) Michigan
	b.	(4)	Kentucky			
	c.	(2)	Florida	Part XV:	a.	(5) West Virginia
	d.	(3)	Indiana		b.	(3) Pennsylvania
					c.	(1) Indiana
Part VI:	a.	(2)	Kentucky		d.	(4) Texas
	b.	(3)	Ohio		e.	(2) Michigan
	c.	(4)	Oregon			
	d.	(1)	Indiana	Part XVI:	a.	(4) South Dakota
					b.	(2) Kentucky
Part VII:	a.	(1)	Louisiana		c.	(3) Pennsylvania
	b.	(3)	Texas		d.	(5) Virginia
	c.	(4)	Wyoming		e.	(1) Florida
	d.	(2)	New York			
				Part XVII:	a.	(4) Mississippi
Part VIII:	a.	(1)	Indiana		b.	(2) Iowa
	b.	(3)	Mississippi		c.	(5) Oregon
	c.	(2)	Kentucky		d.	(1) Colorado
	d.	(4)	Texas		e.	(3) Kentucky
Part IX:	a.	(1)	Connecticut	Part XVIII:	a.	(6) Wisconsin
	b.	(4)	Pennsylvania		b.	(4) Massachusetts
	c.	(2)	Idaho		c.	(2) Illinois
	d.	(3)	Kentucky		d.	(3) Maine
					e.	(1) Arizona
Part X:	a.	(3)	Mississippi		f.	(5) Virginia
	b.	(4)	North Carolina			
	c.	(1)	California	Part XIX:	a.	(3) Montana
	d.	(5)	Wisconsin		b.	(4) Ohio
	e.	(2)	Massachusetts		c.	(1) Arkansas
					d.	(5) Pennsylvania
Part XI:	a.	(1)	Arizona		e.	(2) Kentucky
	b.	(5)	North Carolina		f.	(6) South Carolina
	c.	(4)	Kentucky		g.	(7) West Virginia
	d.	(2)	Arkansas			
	e.	(3)	Colorado	Part XX:	a.	(1) California
					b.	(7) Wisconsin
Part XII:	a.	(2)	Iowa		c.	(2) Colorado
	b.	(5)	New York		d.	(3) Florida
	c.	(4)	Missouri		e.	(4) Illinois
	d.	(3)	Minnesota		f.	(6) Mississippi
	e.	(1)	Colorado		g.	(5) Michigan

86. Part I:
a. (1) California
b. (3) Nevada
c. (5) Utah
d. (6) Wyoming
e. (2) Colorado
f. (4) Oregon

Part II:
a. (3) Idaho
b. (6) Washington
c. (1) Alaska
d. (4) New Mexico
e. (2) Arizona
f. (5) South Dakota

87. Part I:
a. Tennessee
b. Illinois
c. New Jersey
d. Missouri
e. West Virginia
f. North Carolina
g. North Dakota
h. Iowa
i. Kentucky
j. Maryland

Part II:
a. Oklahoma
b. Rhode Island
c. Virginia
d. Vermont
e. Iowa
f. Texas
g. Vermont
h. Rhode Island
i. Virginia
j. Massachusetts

88. Part I:
a. (7) New York (New York City)
b. (6) New Jersey (Atlantic City)
c. (4) Michigan (Battle Creek)
d. (1) Illinois (Chicago)
e. (9) Texas (Dallas)
f. (2) Kentucky (Louisville)
g. (3) Louisiana (New Orleans)

h. (5) Nevada (Reno)
i. (10) Texas (San Antonio)
j. (8) Ohio (Toledo)

Part II:
a. (4) Georgia (Atlanta)
b. (1) Alabama (Birmingham)
c. (8) New York (Buffalo)
d. (9) Ohio (Cincinnati)
e. (2) Colorado (Denver)
f. (6) Michigan (Detroit)
g. (5) Indiana (Gary)
h. (3) Connecticut (Hartford)
i. (7) Missouri (St. Louis)
j. (10) Oklahoma (Tulsa)

89. Part I:
a. (7) Delaware
b. (2) Arizona
c. (10) Hawaii
d. (8) Florida
e. (4) California
f. (9) Georgia
g. (5) Colorado
h. (3) Arkansas
i. (1) Alaska
j. (6) Connecticut

Part II:
a. (3) Indiana
b. (8) Maine
c. (6) Kentucky
d. (1) Idaho
e. (10) Massachusetts
f. (2) Illinois
g. (7) Louisiana
h. (4) Iowa
i. (9) Maryland
j. (5) Kansas

Part III: a. (6) Nebraska
           b. (8) New Hampshire
           c. (2) Minnesota
           d. (5) Montana
           e. (10) New Mexico
           f. (1) Michigan
           g. (7) Nevada
           h. (4) Missouri
           i. (9) New Jersey
           j. (3) Mississippi

Part IV: a. (6) Oregon
           b. (10) South Dakota
           c. (7) Pennsylvania
           d. (1) New York
           e. (9) South Carolina
           f. (5) Oklahoma
           g. (3) North Dakota
           h. (4) Ohio
           i. (8) Rhode Island
           j. (2) North Carolina

Part V: a. (9) Wisconsin
           b. (10) Wyoming
           c. (7) Washington
           d. (2) Tennessee
           e. (6) Virginia
           f. (1) Alabama
           g. (3) Texas
           h. (8) West Virginia
           i. (4) Utah
           j. (5) Vermont

FACTS, FLAGS AND FABLES

1. The first legislative body in America assembled in what future state?

2. Which colony of the original thirteen was not represented at the First Continental Congress in Philadelphia in 1774?

3. On July 4, 1776, all Colonies except one voted to adopt the Declaration of Independence. Which one did not?

4. The oldest federal constitution in existence was framed by a convention of delegates from twelve of the thirteen original states in Philadelphia in May, 1787. Which state failed to send a delegate?

5. Which was the first state to join the Union?

6. The ratification of the conventions of nine states established the Federal Constitution between the States so ratifying. Which state was the ninth to ratify the Constitution?

7. Which of the thirteen original states had its population increase by only 8.3 percent between the start of the War of Independence and the 1970 census?

8. What state has the largest legislature membership?

9. In what state is the oldest public building still standing? (Built in 1610)

10. Where was the first successful oil well in the United States drilled?

11. The first bridge to span the Mississippi River was built between which two states?

12. In which two states is the largest wholly artificial reservoir in the United States?

13. In which states do United States coins with a "D" and a "S" mint mark come from?

14. The town of Ashville in which state had the first all-woman fire department?

15. Near what state did the French freighter Grandcamp explode in 1947, killing 510 persons?

16. What state was the first to pass automobile seat belt legislation?

17. In what state is found the oldest synagogue in America?

18. What state voted to secede from the United States in 1832 if the United States continued to collect tariffs? It backed down when President Jackson prepared for a civil war.

19. In 1776, the constitution of what state gave property-owning women the right to vote in state elections? However, due to the election scandal of 1806, all women were disenfranchised in 1807.

20. Name the state with the most standing covered bridges.

21. Name the state west of the Mississippi River with the most standing covered bridges.

22. The first tax-supported library in the United States was opened at Salisbury in which state?

23. In what state was the disastrous Pocomoke Swamp fire of 1930, which burned the underlying peat for eight months?

24. What is the only state with an official native language?

25. The first United States public school was founded in what state?

26. The passenger dirigible Hindenburg was destroyed in 1933 in what state?

27. What state was the first to have a museum of art, hospital, and scientific society?

28. In what state did the most Revolutionary War battles take place?

29. What state may divide itself into five new states if the people wish?

30. What state has the most one room schools still operating?

31. In 1779, Captain James Cook was killed at what future state?

32. In what state was the Spindletop oil field discovered in 1901?

33. In what state did Nat Turner's Rebellion (1831) take place?

34. In what future state did the Sand Creek Massacre take place in 1864?

35. In what future state did the so-called Pig War take place between the United States and England?

36. In what future state did Bacon's Rebellion take place in 1676?

37. In what future state did the Walker War begin in 1853?

38. In what future state did the Great Swamp fight (1675–King Philip's War) take place?

39. In what state did the Whisky Rebellion (1794) and the Fries Rebellion (1799) take place?

40. In what future state did the battle of Fallen Timbers (1794) take place?

41. In what future state did the Culpeper Rebellion (1677) and the Cary Rebellion (1708) take place?

42. In what future state did the Lincoln County war begin in 1876?

43. In what future state did Shays' Rebellion take place in 1786?

44. In what state did the Aroostook War in 1839 take place?

45. In what state did the Haymarket Riot of 1886 take place?

46. From what future state did Pontiac's Rebellion (1763) take place?

47. In what future state did the Seminole Wars take place?

48. In 1892, the Johnson County War took place in what state?

49. In what state did the Green Corn Rebellion (1917) take place?

50. The so-called Toledo War was a boundary controversy in 1835 between which two states?

51. In what state has the recorded temperature never gone below 0 degrees F?

52. In what state is the deepest well?

53. In what state was the first radio station licensed?

54. Which was the first state to abolish capital punishment?

55. In what four states did or does the United States Mint have facilities?

56. The pheasant was introduced into what state in 1881?

57. Name the first colony (state) to declare its independence from British rule.

58. The earliest parking meter was installed in what state?

59. Which state license plate has a horse and cowboy on it?

60. Name the state where the battle between the Monitor and Merrimac (Virginia) took place.

61. The last of the territory owned in North America by the Spanish was ceded to the United States in 1819. Where was it?

62. Name the first two states that joined the Union after the original thirteen.

63. Which three northern states were invaded by the Confederates during the civil war?

64. Name the two states that were once independent republics.

65. Name the only state that has a unicameral or one-house legislature.

66. What was the first state to definitely proclaim religious toleration?

67. Which entered the United States first as a state—New Mexico or Arizona?

68. Which two states were admitted to the Union on the same date?

69. A certain state endeavored six times to gain statehood and finally succeeded in 1896. Which state was it?

70. Where was Arbor Day first celebrated?

71. In what state was the Comstock Lode?

72. Which was the first state on the Pacific Coast to be admitted to the Union?

73. In what state did the 1905 peace treaty ending the Russo-Japanese War take place?

74. Which state became the first to successfully adopt an income tax?

75. Which state was the first to leave the Union at the beginning of the civil war?

76. Which of the original thirteen states was the last to ratify the Constitution?

77. Which state is the largest supplier of sponges?

78. Paul Revere's famous ride was in which state?

79. Which state is the largest producer of potatoes?

80. Name the states that have been admitted to the Union during the twentieth century. (Since January 1, 1901)

81. Six states were admitted into the Union during Benjamin Harrison's administration. Name them. (1889 and 1890)

82. In what state is Tippecanoe when referring to the slogan, "Tippecanoe and Tyler too?"

83. A peace pipe and Indian shield are on which state flag?

84. Which state flag features a bear?

85. A bison is on which state flag?

86. Upon which state flag is a pelican?

87. There are four state flags that have only two colors. Name the states they represent.

88. Which state flag has three stars in the middle?

89. Which state flag has a white palm tree in the middle?

90. Which state flag is the only one with a green background?

91. This state flag is adapted from the French tricolor, and on the broad central strip is depicted a flying eagle bearing a scroll inscribed, "Our liberties we prize and our rights we will maintain." Name the state.

92. The heraldic device on the quartered flag of this state dates from the founding of the colony. Name the state.

93. The state seal in the center of the flag shows a steamboat ascending the Missouri River, a train steaming towards the Rockies and a blacksmith and a settler's cabin. Name the state.

94. The present state flag is the same as that used during the state's independence. Name the state.

95. This state flag is officially described as, "a crimson cross of St. Andrew on a white field." Name the state.

96. On this yellow state flag the ancient Zia sun-symbol of the Zuni Indians appears in red. Name the state.

97. The canton of this state flag is formed by the British Union flag. Name the state.

98. Which state flies not the usual rectangular flag but a tapering burgee of the national colors?

99. On which state flag is an anchor?

100. What state flag displays the great bear constellation and the pole star?

101. The following are state songs. Name the state they represent.

    a. Home on the Range   (1) Colorado
    b. The Old North State   (2) Connecticut
    c. On the Banks of the Wabash   (3) Florida
       Far Away   (4) Indiana
    d. Where the Columbines Grow   (5) Kansas
    e. Suwannee River   (6) North Carolina
    f. Yankee Doodle

102. Which states are most likely to be associated with the following names—either factual or legendary?

    Part I: a. Daniel Boone   (1) California
                  b. Joaquin Murrieta   (2) Florida
                  c. Ponce de Leon   (3) Hawaii
                  d. Kamehameha   (4) Illinois
                  e. Mrs. O'Leary   (5) Kentucky
                  f. Evangeline   (6) Lousiana
                  g. Priscilla Mullens and   (7) Massachusetts
                     John Alden   (8) Minnesota
                  h. Paul Bunyan

Part II:

a.	John Henry	(1) Missouri
b.	Pecos Bill	(2) New Jersey
c.	Benjamin Franklin	(3) North Carolina
d.	Virginia Dare	(4) Ohio
e.	Jesse James	(5) Pennsylvania
f.	Molly Pitcher	(6) South Carolina
g.	Johnny Appleseed	(7) Texas
h.	Francis Marion (Swamp Fox)	(8) Vermont
i.	Ethan Allen	(9) West Virginia

103. Most of the action in the following books takes place in a specific state. Match the state to the book.

Part I:

a.	*Ramona* (1884), by Helen Hunt Jackson	(1) Alabama
b.	*The Story of a Bad Boy*, by Thomas Bailey Aldrich	(2) California
c.	*The Pit* (1903), by Frank Norris	(3) Florida
d.	*To Kill a Mockingbird*, by Harper Lee	(4) Illinois
e.	*Giant*, by Edna Ferber	(5) New Hampshire
f.	*The Yearling* (1938), by Marjorie Kinnan Rawlings	(6) Texas

Part II:

a.	*Guys and Dolls* (1950), by Damon Runyan	(1) Alaska
b.	*Ice Palace* (1958), by Edna Ferber	(2) Georgia
c.	*Tobacco Road* (1932), by Erskine Caldwell	(3) Kansas
d.	*Sartoris* (1929), by William Faulkner	(4) Mississippi
e.	*Death Comes to the Archbishop*, by Willa Cather	(5) New Mexico
f.	*In Cold Blood* (1966), by Truman Capote	(6) New York

104. Match the largest production item to the state.

Part I:

a.	Bourbon	(1) Arizona
b.	Copper	(2) Colorado
c.	Molybdenum	(3) Florida
d.	Silver	(4) Idaho
e.	Phosphate	(5) Kentucky

Part II: a. Sulphur   (1) Illinois
            b. Musical Instruments   (2) Indiana
            c. Fluorospar   (3) Kansas
            d. Wheat   (4) Louisiana
            e. Lead   (5) Missouri

Part III: a. Nickel   (1) Nebraska
            b. Dairy products   (2) New Mexico
            c. Alfalfa   (3) Oregon
            d. Asphalt   (4) Texas
            e. Potash   (5) Wisconsin

105. In which states did the following fairs and expositions take place?

    a. 1853 – Crystal Palace Exposition
    b. 1876 – Centennial Exposition
    c. 1893 – World's Columbian Exposition
    d. 1904 – Louisiana Purchase Exposition
    e. 1905 – Lewis and Clark Centennial Exposition
    f. 1915-16 – Panama-Pacific International Exposition
    g. 1962 – The Century 21 Exposition
    h. 1982 – World's Fair

    (1) California (San Francisco)
    (2) Illinois (Chicago)
    (3) Missouri (St. Louis)
    (4) New York (New York City)
    (5) Oregon (Portland)
    (6) Pennsylvania (Philadelphia)
    (7) Tennessee (Knoxville)
    (8) Washington (Seattle)

ANSWERS TO
FACTS, FLAGS AND FABLES

1. Virgina (met at Jamestown in 1619)
2. Georgia
3. New York
4. Rhode Island
5. Delaware (December 7, 1787)
6. New Hampshire
7. New Hampshire
8. New Hampshire (about 400 members)
9. New Mexico (Santa Fe – Palace of the Governors)
10. Pennsylvania (near Titusville in 1859)
11. Iowa (Davenport) and Illinois (Rock Island)
12. Arizona and Nevada (Lake Mead)
13. Colorado (Denver) and California (San Francisco)
14. New York
15. Texas
16. Illinois (1955)
17. Rhode Island
18. South Carolina
19. New Jersey
20. Pennsylvania (more than 200)
21. Oregon (about 50)
22. Connecticut
23. Delaware
24. Hawaii
25. Massachusetts
26. New Jersey (Lakehurst)
27. Pennsylvania (Philadelphia Academy of Arts, The Pennsylvania Hospital, The Franklin Institute)
28. South Carolina (about 137)
29. Texas
30. Nebraska
31. Hawaii
32. Texas
33. Virginia
34. Colorado
35. Washington
36. Virginia
37. Utah
38. Rhode Island
39. Pennsylvania
40. Ohio
41. North Carolina
42. New Mexico
43. Massachusetts
44. Maine
45. Illinois
46. Illinois
47. Florida
48. Wyoming
49. Oklahoma
50. Michigan and Ohio
51. Hawaii (lowest recorded–12 degrees F in 1979)

52. Oklahoma (Gas well, Washita County – 31,411 feet)

53. Pennsylvania (KDKA Pittsburgh – 1920)

54. Michigan (1847)

55. California (San Francisco), Colorado (Denver), New York (West Point), Pennsylvania (Philadelphia)

56. Oregon

57. New Hampshire

58. Oklahoma (Oklahoma City in 1935)

59. Wyoming

60. Virginia

61. Florida

62. Vermont (1791) and Kentucky (1792)

63. Indiana, Ohio and Pennsylvania

64. Texas and Vermont (declared independence in 1777 under the name of New Connecticut)

65. Nebraska

66. Maryland (called the Free State of Maryland)

67. New Mexico

68. North and South Dakota (November 2, 1889)

69. Utah

70. Nebraska (April 10, 1872)

71. Nevada

72. California (1850)

73. New Hampshire (Portsmouth)

74. Wisconsin (1911)

75. South Carolina

76. Rhode Island (1790)

77. Florida

78. Massachusetts

79. Idaho

80. Alaska, Arizona, Hawaii, New Mexico, Oklahoma

81. Idaho, Montana, North Dakota, South Dakota, Washington, Wyoming

82. Indiana

83. Oklahoma

84. California

85. Wyoming

86. Louisiana

87. Alabama, Alaska, New Mexico, South Carolina

88. Tennessee

89. South Carolina

90. Washington

91. Iowa

92. Maryland

93. Nebraska

94. Texas

95. Alabama

96. New Mexico

97. Hawaii

98. Ohio

99. Rhode Island

100. Alaska

101. a. (5) Kansas
   b. (6) North Carolina
   c. (4) Indiana
   d. (1) Colorado
   e. (3) Florida
   f. (2) Connecticut

102. Part I: a. (5) Kentucky
b. (1) California
c. (2) Florida
d. (3) Hawaii
e. (4) Illinois
f. (6) Lousiana
g. (7) Massachusetts
h. (8) Minnesota

     Part II: a. (9) West Virginia
b. (7) Texas
c. (5) Pennsylvania
d. (3) North Carolina
e. (1) Missouri
f. (2) New Jersey
g. (4) Ohio
h. (6) South Carolina
i. (8) Vermont

103. Part I: a. (2) California
b. (5) New Hampshire
c. (4) Illinois
d. (1) Alabama
e. (6) Texas
f. (3) Florida

     Part II: a. (6) New York
b. (1) Alaska
c. (2) Georgia
d. (4) Mississippi
e. (5) New Mexico
f. (3) Kansas

104. Part I: a. (5) Kentucky
b. (1) Arizona
c. (2) Colorado
d. (4) Idaho
e. (3) Florida

     Part II: a. (4) Louisiana
b. (2) Indiana
c. (1) Illinois
d. (3) Kansas
e. (5) Missouri

     Part III: a. (3) Oregon
b. (5) Wisconsin
c. (1) Nebraska
d. (4) Texas
e. (2) New Mexico

105. a. (4) New
b. (6) Pennsylvania
c. (2) Illinois
d. (3) Missouri
e. (5) Oregon
f. (1) California
g. (8) Washington
h. (7) Tennessee

GEOLOGY AND GEOGRAPHY

1. In what state is the longest undammed river of the United States?

2. The largest desert in the United States is the Chihuahuan. It extends into what three states?

3. In what state is the lowest point (elevation) of land?

4. The highest natural arch in the world is in what state?

5. Sutter Buttes are sometimes called the smallest mountain range in the United States. In what state are they located?

6. In what state can be found the tallest sand dunes in North America?

7. What state has more than a quarter of all the country's major springs?

8. The world's greatest salt deposits are in what state?

9. In what state is North America's only diamond mine?

10. One of the world's notable natural features is the Old Man of the Mountains. In what state is it located?

11. In what state is found the nation's only major east-west mountain range?

12. In what state is the largest natural lake west of the Mississippi River?

13. The world record total production of a single gold mine is the Homestake Mine. In what state is it located?

14. In what state is the Shenandoah Valley?

15. What is the westernmost state?

16. What state is the most southerly?

17. Alaska is the most northerly of the fifty states. What state is the next most northerly?

18. Liberty Island, home of the Statue of Liberty, is in what states?

19. The largest volcano of the 48 contiguous states is located in what state?

20. The mountains in this state have given it the loftiest average height east of the Rockies. Name it.

21. What state has the largest United States coal reserves?

22. In what state is the largest volcano?

23. In what state is found the world's largest flat top mesa?

24. What state has the largest inland body of saltwater?

25. In the northeast corner of what present-day state was the Grand Portage located? It was a nine mile overland haul between a lake and a river.

26. In what state is the Matanuska Valley?

27. The San Juan Islands are part of which state?

28. In what state do the Jefferson, Gallatin and Madison rivers come together to form the Missouri River.

29. The continental divide is part of which five states?

30. Other then California, what other state has land below sea level?

31. There are more than 90 named summits in the United States over 14,000 feet above sea level. They are located in only four states. Name the states.

32. The strongest earthquake to ever hit North America occurred closest to what state?

33. Of the forty-eight contiguous states, which is the westernmost?

34. In what state is the geographic center of the North American continent?

35. In what state is the geographic center of the United States?

36. In what state is the geographic center of the forty-eight contiguous states?

37. Of the forty-eight contiguous states which one has the most tidal shoreline?

38. Of the forty-eight contiguous states which one has most of the high mountain peaks?

39. The highest sea cliffs in the world are found in which state?

40. Chimney Rock (along the Oregon trail) is in which state?

41. In what state are the Finger Lakes?

42. The Mojave Desert is located mainly in which two states?

43. In what state is Stone Mountain (memorial carving in Stone Mountain Park)?

44. In what state is the Salton Sea?

45. Pikes Peak is in which state?

46. In what state is the deepest United States lake?

47. In what state are the Boston Mountains?

48. The Grand Canyon is in which state?

49. New England's highest peak is in which state?

50. Where is Diamond Head?

51. Monument Valley is in which two states?

52. In what state is the Black Rock Desert?

53. What state has the lowest high point altitude?

54. What state has the highest low point altitude?

55. In what state is the largest known underground chamber in the world?

56. In what state is the highest waterfall in the United States?

57. Where in the United States is there a rain forest?

58. In what state is Lake Okeechobee?

59. In what state is the highest mountain in the Appalachian system?

60. In what state are the Alabama Hills?

61. Grasshopper Glacier is found in which state?

62. The following are names of Mountain Ranges:
    a. The White Mountains are found in what three states?
    b. The Green Mountains are found in what two states?
    c. The Blue Mountains are found in what three states?
    d. The Black Mountain Range is found in which state?

63. Three states claim to have the shortest river in the world. The river's names are D River, Roe River and Malad River. Name the states.

64. The thunderegg is the official state rock of which state?

65. The following is a list of state gems. Match the state to the gem.

    a. Turquoise   (1) Colorado
    b. Jade   (2) Michigan
    c. Isle Royal greenstone   (3) Nebraska
    d. Emerald   (4) New Mexico
    e. Aquamarine   (5) North Carolina
    f. Petrified wood   (6) South Dakota
    g. Blue agate   (7) Washington
    h. Fairburn agate   (8) Wyoming

66. Match the following bays and sounds to the state they are adjacent to.

a. Pamlico Sound   (1) California
b. Apalachee Bay   (2) Florida
c. Puget Sound   (3) Massachusetts
d. Morro Bay   (4) Michigan
e. Matagorda Bay   (5) North Carolina
f. St. Helena Sound   (6) South Carolina
g. Saginaw Bay   (7) Texas
h. Weymouth Bay   (8) Washington

67. In what states are the following dunes?

a. Imperial Sand Dunes   (1) California
b. Coral Pink Sand Dunes State Park   (2) Colorado
       (3) Idaho
c. Monahans Sandhill State Park   (4) Michigan
d. White Sands National Monument   (5) New Mexico
       (6) North Carolina
e. Sleeping Bear Dunes National Lakeshore   (7) Texas
       (8) Utah
f. Jockey's Ridge State Park
g. Bruneau Dunes State Park
h. Great Sand Dunes National Monument

68. In what states are the following gorges and canyons?

a. Black Canyon   (1) Arizona
b. Walnut Canyon   (2) California
c. Topanga Canyon   (3) Colorado
d. Delaware Water Gap   (4) Nevada
e. Columbia River Gorge   (5) New Mexico
f. Big Stone Gap   (6) Oregon-Washington
g. Chaco Canyon   (7) Pennsylvania
h. The Dells   (8) Texas
i. Palo Duro Canyon   (9) West Virginia
j. Floyds Canyon   (10) Wisconsin

69. Name the states in which the following natural lakes (all more than 100 square miles) are located.

a.	Flathead	(1) Alaska
b.	Iliamna	(2) Alaska
c.	Leech	(3) Idaho
d.	Moosehead	(4) Louisiana
e.	Pend Oreille	(5) Maine
f.	Pontchartrain	(6) Minnesota
g.	Upper Klamath	(7) Montana
h.	Winnebago	(8) Oregon
i.	Yellowstone	(9) Wisconsin
j.	Clark	(10) Wyoming

70. In what states are the following islands?

Part I:

a.	Santa Catalina Island	(1) California
b.	Key Largo	(2) Florida
c.	Mackinac Island	(3) Georgia
d.	Martha's Vineyard	(4) Louisiana
e.	Sapelo Island	(5) Massachusetts
f.	Marsh Island	(6) Michigan

Part II:

a.	Roanoke Island	(1) Alaska
b.	Tangier Island	(2) Hawaii
c.	South Padre Island	(3) Texas
d.	Admiralty Island	(4) North Carolina
e.	Kahoolawe	(5) Virginia
f.	Orcas Island	(6) Washington

71. In what states are the source or upper limit of length of the following rivers?

Part I:

a.	Hudson	(1) Alaska
b.	Klamath	(2) Nebraska
c.	Republican	(3) New Mexico
d.	North Canadian	(4) New York
e.	Snake	(5) Ohio
f.	Wabash	(6) Oregon
g.	Savannah	(7) South Carolina
h.	Porcupine	(8) Wyoming

Part II: a. Brazos   (1) Indiana
             b. Connecticut   (2) Kansas
             c. Illinois   (3) Maryland
             d. Mississippi   (4) Minnesota
             e. Osage   (5) Mississippi
             f. Tombigbee   (6) Missouri
             g. St. Francis   (7) New Hampshire
             h. Potomac   (8) Texas

72. In what states may be found the following waterfalls?

Part I: a. Feather Falls   (1) California
             b. Snoqualmie Falls   (2) Colorado
             c. Toccoa Falls   (3) Georgia
             d. Issaqueena Falls   (4) Idaho
             e. Shoshone Falls   (5) South Carolina
             f. Seven Falls   (6) Washington

Part II: a. Blackwater Falls   (1) Massachusetts
             b. Multnomah Falls   (2) Minnesota
             c. Gooseberry Falls   (3) New Hampshire
             d. Bellows Falls   (4) Oregon
             e. Arethusa Falls   (5) Vermont
             f. Wahconah Falls   (6) West Virginia

Part III: a. Bushkill Falls   (1) Arizona
             b. Havasu Falls   (2) Michigan
             c. Tahquamenon Falls   (3) North Carolina
             d. Hickory Nut Falls   (4) Pennsylvania
             e. Crabtree Falls   (5) Tennessee
             f. Foster Falls   (6) Virginia

73. In what states are the following caves?

Part I: a. Lehman Caves   (1) Alabama
             b. Mitchell Caverns   (2) California
             c. DeSoto Caverns   (3) Colorado
             d. Ruby Falls-Lookout   (4) Kentucky
                Mountain Caverns   (5) Nevada
             e. Mammoth Cave   (6) New York
             f. Timpanogos Cave   (7) Tennessee
             g. Cave of the Winds   (8) Utah
             h. Howe Caverns

Part II:

a.	Mystery Cave	(1)	Arkansas
b.	Jewel Cave	(2)	Indiana
c.	Carlsbad Caverns	(3)	Minnesota
d.	Cave of the Mounds	(4)	Missouri
e.	Wyandotte Caves	(5)	New Mexico
f.	Olentangy Indian Caverns	(6)	Ohio
g.	Blanchard Spring Caverns	(7)	South Dakota
h.	Meramec Caverns	(8)	Wisconsin

Part III:

a.	Caverns of Sonora	(1)	Hawaii
b.	Luray Caverns	(2)	Idaho
c.	Smoke Hole Caverns	(3)	Montana
d.	Lewis and Clark Caverns	(4)	Oregon
e.	Minnetonka Cave	(5)	Texas
f.	Lava River Cave	(6)	Virginia
g.	Gardner Cave	(7)	Washington
h.	Kaumana Caves	(8)	West Virginia

74. United States Forest Service scenic byways are listed. Give the state they are located in.

Part I:

a.	Mesa Falls Scenic Byway	(1)	Arizona
b.	Coronado Trail	(2)	Arkansas
c.	Sylamore Scenic Byway	(3)	California
d.	Longleaf Trail Scenic Byway	(4)	Idaho
e.	Bighorn Scenic Byways	(5)	Kentucky
f.	Carson Pass Scenic Highway	(6)	Louisiana
g.	Mount Rogers Scenic Byway	(7)	Virginia
h.	Zilpo Road	(8)	Wyoming

Part II:

a.	Russell-Brasstown Scenic Byway	(1)	Colorado
b.	Whitefish Bay Scenic Byway	(2)	Georgia
c.	San Juan Skyway	(3)	Michigan
d.	Logan Canyon Highway	(4)	Montana
e.	McKenzie-Santiam Pass Loop	(5)	New Mexico
f.	Wise River-Polaris Road	(6)	Oregon
g.	Sandia Crest Road	(7)	Utah

Part III:

a. Great Divide Highway
b. Kancamagus Highway
c. Apalachee Savannahs Scenic Byway
d. Ocoee Scenic Byway
e. Forest Heritage Scenic Byway
f. Glade Top Trail
g. Spearfish Canyon Highway
h. Highland Scenic Byway

(1) Florida
(2) Missouri
(3) New Hampshire
(4) North Carolina
(5) South Dakota
(6) Tennessee
(7) West Virginia
(8) Wisconsin

75. Each state has a high elevation point. Match the states with their highest point.

Part I:

a. Mount Greylock
b. Clingmans Dome
c. Guadalupe Peak
d. Wheeler Peak
e. Black Mesa
f. Spruce Knob
g. Mount Mansfield
h. Brasstown Bald
i. Mount Katahdin
j. Mount Sunflower

(1) Georgia
(2) Kansas
(3) Maine
(4) Massachusetts
(5) New Mexico
(6) Oklahoma
(7) Tennessee
(8) Texas
(9) Vermont
(10) West Virginia

Part II:

a. Woodall Mountain
b. Charles Mound
c. Campbell Hill
d. Mt. Frissell
e. Boundary Peak
f. Driskill Mountain
g. White Butte
h. Jerimoth Hill
i. Mt. Arvon
j. Mt. Davis

(1) Connecticut
(2) Louisiana
(3) Illinois
(4) Michigan
(5) Mississippi
(6) Nevada
(7) North Dakota
(8) Ohio
(9) Pennsylvania
(10) Rhode Island

Part III:

a. Borah Peak	(1)	Colorado
b. Mount Elbert	(2)	Idaho
c. Mount Marcy	(3)	Kentucky
d. Mount Rainier	(4)	Maryland
e. Blackbone Mountain	(5)	Missouri
f. Sassafras Mountain	(6)	New York
g. Gannett Peak	(7)	South Carolina
h. Taum Sauk Mount	(8)	Washington
i. Black Mountain	(9)	Wisconsin
j. Timms Hill	(10)	Wyoming

Part IV:

a. Mount Hood	(1)	Alabama
b. Magazine Mountain	(2)	Arizona
c. Cheaha Mountain	(3)	Arkansas
d. Mount Whitney	(4)	California
e. Harney Peak	(5)	Minnesota
f. Granite Peak	(6)	Montana
g. Eagle Mountain	(7)	Oregon
h. Humphrey's Peak	(8)	South Dakota
i. Mount Rogers	(9)	Utah
j. Kings Peak	(10)	Virginia

ANSWERS TO
GEOLOGY AND GEOGRAPHY

1. Alaska (Yukon River)
2. Arizona, New Mexico, Texas
3. California (Death Valley – 282 feet below sea level)
4. Utah (Rainbow Bridge)
5. California
6. Colorado (Great Sand Dunes – up to 700 feet high)
7. Florida
8. Kansas (Hutchison)
9. Arkansas (near Murfreesboro)
10. New Hampshire
11. Utah (Uintas)
12. Utah (Great Salt Lake)
13. South Dakota
14. Virginia
15. Alaska
16. Hawaii
17. Minnesota
18. New Jersey and New York
19. California (Mt. Shasta)
20. West Virginia
21. Wyoming
22. Hawaii (Mauna Kea)
23. Colorado (Grand Mesa)
24. Utah (Great Salt Lake)
25. Minnesota
26. Alaska
27. Washington
28. Montana
29. Montana, Idaho, Wyoming, Colorado, New Mexico
30. Louisiana (New Orleans – 8 feet below sea level)
31. Alaska, California, Colorado, Washington
32. Alaska (80 miles east of Anchorage in 1964 – registered 9.2 on the Richter scale)
33. Washington (Cape Alava)
34. North Dakota (Pierce County)
35. South Dakota (Butte County)
36. Kansas (Smith County)
37. Louisiana
38. Colorado
39. Hawaii (near Unilehi Point – descends 3,300 feet to the sea with an average gradient of more than 55 degrees)
40. Nebraska
41. New York
42. Arizona and California
43. Georgia
44. California
45. Colorado
46. Oregon (Crater Lake)
47. Arkansas
48. Arizona
49. New Hampshire (Mt. Washington)
50. Hawaii
51. Arizona and Utah
52. Nevada
53. Florida (345 feet above sea level)

54. Colorado (3,350 feet above sea level)

55. New Mexico (the Big Room of the Carlsbad Caverns – 4,270 feet long, 328 feet high, 656 feet wide)

56. California (Ribbon Falls in Yosemite National Park – 1,612 feet. Upper Yosemite Falls are 1,430 feet)

57. Washington

58. Florida

59. North Carolina (Mt. Mitchell)

60. California

61. Montana (millions of grasshoppers are embedded in the ice of the glacier)

62. a. California, Nevada, New Hampshire
    b. Massachusetts, Vermont
    c. Oregon, Pennsylvania, Washington
    d. North Carolina

63. Oregon (D River), Montana (Roe River), Idaho (Malad River)

64. Oregon

65. a. (4) New Mexico
    b. (8) Wyoming
    c. (2) Michigan
    d. (5) North Carolina
    e. (1) Colorado
    f. (7) Washington
    g. (3) Nebraska
    h. (6) South Dakota

66. a. (5) North Carolina
    b. (2) Florida
    c. (8) Washington
    d. (1) California
    e. (7) Texas
    f. (6) South Carolina
    g. (4) Michigan
    h. (3) Massachusetts

67. a. (1) California (Brawley)
    b. (8) Utah (Kanab)
    c. (7) Texas (Monahans)
    d. (5) New Mexico
    e. (4) Michigan
    f. (6) North Carolina (Nags Head)
    g. (3) Idaho
    h. (2) Colorado

68. a. (3) Colorado
    b. (1) Arizona
    c. (2) California
    d. (7) Pennsylvania
    e. (6) Oregon-Washington
    f. (9) West Virginia
    g. (5) New Mexico
    h. (10) Wisconsin
    i. (8) Texas
    j. (4) Nevada

69. a. (7) Montana
    b. (1) Alaska
    c. (6) Minnesota
    d. (5) Maine
    e. (3) Idaho
    f. (4) Louisiana
    g. (8) Oregon
    h. (9) Wisconsin
    i. (10) Wyoming
    j. (2) Alaska

70. Part I: a. (1) California
    b. (2) Florida
    c. (6) Michigan
    d. (5) Massachusetts
    e. (3) Georgia
    f. (4) Louisiana

    Part II: a. (4) North Carolina
    b. (5) Virginia
    c. (3) Texas
    d. (1) Alaska
    e. (2) Hawaii
    f. (6) Washington

71. Part I:
   a. (4) New York
   b. (6) Oregon
   c. (2) Nebraska
   d. (3) New Mexico
   e. (8) Wyoming
   f. (5) Ohio
   g. (7) South Carolina
   h. (1) Alaska

   Part II:
   a. (8) Texas
   b. (7) New Hampshire
   c. (1) Indiana
   d. (4) Minnesota
   e. (2) Kansas
   f. (5) Mississippi
   g. (6) Missouri
   h. (3) Maryland

72. Part I:
   a. (1) California
   b. (6) Washington
   c. (3) Georgia
   d. (5) South Carolina
   e. (4) Idaho
   f. (2) Colorado

   Part II:
   a. (6) West Virginia
   b. (4) Oregon
   c. (2) Minnesota
   d. (5) Vermont
   e. (3) New Hampshire
   f. (1) Massachusetts

   Part III:
   a. (4) Pennsylvania
   b. (1) Arizona
   c. (2) Michigan
   d. (3) North Carolina
   e. (6) Virginia
   f. (5) Tennessee

73. Part I:
   a. (5) Nevada
   b. (2) California
   c. (1) Alabama
   d. (7) Tennessee
   e. (4) Kentucky
   f. (8) Utah
   g. (3) Colorado
   h. (6) New York

Part II:
   a. (3) Minnesota
   b. (7) South Dakota
   c. (5) New Mexico
   d. (8) Wisconsin
   e. (2) Indiana
   f. (6) Ohio
   g. (1) Arkansas
   h. (4) Missouri

Part III:
   a. (5) Texas
   b. (6) Virginia
   c. (8) West Virginia
   d. (3) Montana
   e. (2) Idaho
   f. (4) Oregon
   g. (7) Washington
   h. (1) Hawaii

74. Part I:
   a. (4) Idaho
   b. (1) Arizona
   c. (2) Arkansas
   d. (6) Louisiana
   e. (8) Wyoming
   f. (3) California
   g. (7) Virginia
   h. (5) Kentucky

   Part II:
   a. (2) Georgia
   b. (3) Michigan
   c. (1) Colorado
   d. (7) Utah
   e. (6) Oregon
   f. (4) Montana
   g. (5) New Mexico

   Part III:
   a. (8) Wisconsin
   b. (3) New Hampshire
   c. (1) Florida
   d. (6) Tennessee
   e. (4) North Carolina
   f. (2) Missouri
   g. (5) South Dakota
   h. (7) West Virginia

75. Part I:
  a. (4) Massachusetts
  b. (7) Tennessee
  c. (8) Texas
  d. (5) New Mexico
  e. (6) Oklahoma
  f. (10) West Virginia
  g. (9) Vermont
  h. (1) Georgia
  i. (3) Maine
  j. (2) Kansas

Part II:
  a. (5) Mississippi
  b. (3) Illinois
  c. (8) Ohio
  d. (1) Connecticut
  e. (6) Nevada
  f. (2) Louisiana
  g. (7) North Dakota
  h. (10) Rhode Island
  i. (4) Michigan
  j. (9) Pennsylvania

Part III:
  a. (2) Idaho
  b. (1) Colorado
  c. (6) New York
  d. (8) Washington
  e. (4) Maryland
  f. (7) South Carolina
  g. (10) Wyoming
  h. (5) Missouri
  i. (3) Kentucky
  j. (9) Wisconsin

Part IV:
  a. (7) Oregon
  b. (3) Arkansas
  c. (1) Alabama
  d. (4) California
  e. (8) South Dakota
  f. (6) Montana
  g. (5) Minnesota
  h. (2) Arizona
  i. (10) Virginia
  j. (9) Utah

LISTS AND LAND

1. In 1789, what state ceded land for the United States Capital?

2. In 1862, Daniel Freeman was the nation's first recipient of land granted under the Homestead Act. In what future state?

3. What future state seceded from New York territory in 1777?

4. In 1863, West Virginia was made a separate state from the territory of what other state?

5. Although historians disagree as to the route of the 1540-42 Coronado Expedition, several include the area traveled in what five present day states?

6. The Butterfield Overland mail route crossed through what seven present day states?

7. The Louisiana Purchase from France in 1803, included all or some of the areas in thirteen future states. Name them.

8. The Mexican Cession of 1848 included all or some of the areas in seven future states. Name them.

9. The Oregon Country, acquired by treaty with Great Britain in 1846 included all or some of the areas in five future states. Name them.

10. On a clear day one can see five states from atop the Empire State building in New York City. Name them.

11. When completed the North Country National Scenic Trail will extend approximately 3,200 miles through which states?

12. In what states are the termini of the following recreation trails?
    a. Appalachian Trail
    b. Pacific Crest Trail
    c. Continental Divide Trail

13. What is the only inland state in New England?

14. Of the forty-eight contiguous states, which one has the most public land?

15. Name the eleven Confederate states.

16. Name the six New England states.

17. The Oregon Trail crossed areas of at least six future states. Name them.

18. From what two future states did most of the pioneers branch off from the Oregon Trail to California?

19. The Lewis and Clark Expedition (Corps of Discovery) traveled through what is today parts of ten states. Name them.

20. The Barlow Road portion of the Oregon Trail is in what state?

21. The Hudspeth cutoff on the Oregon Trail was located in what future state?

22. The Sublette cutoff on the Oregon Trail was located in what future state?

23. The original highway Route 66 went from Chicago to Los Angeles through what eight states?

24. The Santa Fe Trail crossed an area within five future states. Name them.

25. Name the original thirteen colonies (states).

26. In what states are the termini of the following historic roads and trails?
    a. Santa Fe Trail
    b. Chisholm Trail
    c. Oregon Trail
    d. Pony Express Trail
    e. Butterfield Overland Trail
    f. Natchez Trail
    g. Morman Trail
    h. Bozeman Trail
    i. Cheyenne-Deadwood Trail
    j. Mullan Road

27. The Gadsden Purchase incorporated areas of which two future states?

28. The Cherokee strip was land opened by the government. In what state is it now?

29. The original range of the American Indian tribe listed, covered areas within the boundaries of one or more future states. Name at least one state for each tribe's range.
    a. Catawba
    b. Comanche
    c. Crow
    d. Modoc
    e. Pawnee
    f. Potawatomi
    g. Sac and Fox
    h. Seneca

30. More the 50 percent of land in four states is federally owned. Name them.

31. What state has the largest percentage of its land under the jurisdiction of the Bureau of Land Management?

32. Which ten states have two words in their name?

33. Name the four states that start and end with the same letter.

34. Name the eight states that begin with the letter *M*.

35. Name the eight states that begin with the letter *N*.

36. The 48 contiguous states are divided into four time zones. Arrange the four states listed by the following time zones: (1) Eastern, (2) Central, (3) Mountain, and (4) Pacific.
    a. Minnesota, Georgia, Nevada, Montana
    b. Arizona, Oregon, Alabama, Ohio
    c. Texas, New Mexico, California, Florida

37. Each of the four states listed is either north, east, south or west of the others. Starting with the northernmost state, list them in correct clockwise order.
    a. Kansas, South Dakota, Wyoming, Iowa
    b. Arkansas, West Virginia, Wisconsin, Utah
    c. Nebraska, Maine, Maryland, Minnesota
    d. Wyoming, Texas, Arizona, Missouri
    e. Massachusetts, Pennsylvania, Delaware, Vermont

38. Numerals on the left represent the first number of the ten main Zip Code National Areas. Ten states are listed. Match the state to the first number of its Zip Code. (For example, the number '8' is the first number of the Zip Codes in Colorado.)

0	(1)	Illinois
1	(2)	Louisiana
2	(3)	Michigan
3	(4)	Montana
4	(5)	Nevada
5	(6)	Pennsylvania
6	(7)	Rhode Island
7	(8)	South Carolina
8	(9)	Tennessee
9	(10)	Washington

39. North-South Interstate highways are odd numbered. Four states are named with an Interstate number. The route goes through parts of three of them. Which state doesn't it enter?
    a. I-15 .... Idaho, Nevada, Arizona, New Mexico
    b. I-25 .... New Mexico, Colorado, Wyoming, Montana
    c. I-35 .... Kansas, Nebraska, Iowa, Minnesota
    d. I-55 .... Indiana, Illinois, Arkansas, Missouri
    e. I-75 .... Kentucky, Tennessee, Alabama, Michigan
    f. I-95 .... Maryland, West Virginia, North Carolina, Florida

40. East-West Interstate highways are even numbered. Four states are named with an Interstate number. The route goes through parts of three of them. Which state doesn't it enter?
    a. I-10 .... Georgia, Louisiana, Arizona, Alabama
    b. I-20 .... North Carolina, South Carolina, Alabama, Texas
    c. I-40 .... California, Oklahoma, Arkansas, Mississippi
    d. I-70 .... Colorado, Nebraska, Missouri, Ohio
    e. I-80 .... Nevada, Wyoming, Colorado, Iowa
    f. I-90 .... Montana, North Dakota, Minnesota, Pennsylvania

41. In which states are the following National Wildlife Refuges?

    Part I:
    a. Chincoteague
    b. Pea Island
    c. Agassiz
    d. De Soto
    e. Sabine
    f. Sequoyah

    (1) Iowa
    (2) Louisiana
    (3) Minnesota
    (4) North Carolina
    (5) Oklahoma
    (6) Virginia

    Part II:
    a. Charles M. Russell
    b. Hart Mountain
    c. Kenai
    d. Nisqually
    e. Kofa
    f. Brigantine

    (1) Alaska
    (2) Arizona
    (3) Montana
    (4) New Jersey
    (5) Oregon
    (6) Washington

    Part III:
    a. Great Dismal Swamp
    b. Modoc
    c. Stillwater
    d. Camas
    e. Browns Park
    f. Muleshoe

    (1) California
    (2) Colorado
    (3) Idaho
    (4) Nevada
    (5) Texas
    (6) Virginia

42. Match the following wilderness areas with the states listed.

    Part I:
        a. Marble Mountain Wilderness   (1) Alabama
        b. Kalmiopsis Wilderness   (2) California
        c. Mount Baker Wilderness   (3) New Mexico
        d. Chama Wilderness   (4) Oregon
        e. Indian Mounds Wilderness Area   (5) Texas
        f. Sipsey Wilderness   (6) Washington

    Part II:
        a. Headwaters Wilderness Area   (1) Colorado
        b. Great Gulf Wilderness   (2) Minnesota
        c. Boundary Waters Canoe Area   (3) Nebraska
            Wilderness   (4) New Hampshire
        d. Soldier Creek Wilderness   (5) Utah
        e. Flat Top Wilderness   (6) Wisconsin
        f. High Uintas Wilderness

    Part III:
        a. Popo Agie Wilderness Area   (1) Idaho
        b. Bob Marshall Wilderness   (2) Indiana
        c. Gospel-Hump Wilderness   (3) Michigan
        d. Porcupine Mountains Wilderness   (4) Montana
        e. Charles C. Deam Wilderness   (5) Nevada
        f. Ruby Mountains Wilderness   (6) Wyoming

43. In which states are the following National Forests?

    Part I:
        a. Mark Twain   (1) California
        b. Humboldt   (2) Missouri
        c. Angelina   (3) Nevada
        d. Willamette   (4) Oregon
        e. Allegheny   (5) Pennsylvania
        f. Mendocino   (6) South Carolina
        g. Francis Marion   (7) Texas
        h. Gifford Pinchot   (8) Washington

    Part II:
        a. Chippewa   (1) Alaska
        b. Lincoln   (2) Arizona
        c. Fishlake   (3) Minnesota
        d. Lewis and Clark   (4) Montana
        e. Tongass   (5) New Mexico
        f. Coconino   (6) North Carolina
        g. Pisgah   (7) Utah
        h. Nicolet   (8) Wisconsin

Part III:

a. Wayne
b. Shawnee
c. Ozark
d. Cherokee
e. Bankhead
f. Homochitto
g. Kisatchie
h. Targhee

(1) Alabama
(2) Arkansas
(3) Idaho
(4) Illinois
(5) Louisiana
(6) Mississippi
(7) Ohio
(8) Tennessee

44. Portions of which five states are considered to be in the Ohio Valley?

NOTE: The following questions (45-50) do not necessarily have an absolute correct or complete answer. Variances may occur, depending on what reference is used.

45. What seven states comprise the area known as the "Deep South?"

46. Which six states are part of the "Piedmont Plateau?"

47. Which five states are sometimes known as the "Middle West" states?

48. What eight states are sometimes known as the "Mountain states?"

49. Which seven states comprise the so-called "Hillbilly" country?

50. The term "Eleven Western States," refers to which contiguous states?

ANSWERS TO
LISTS AND LAND

1. Maryland

2. Nebraska

3. Vermont

4. Virginia

5. Arizona, Kansas, New Mexico, Oklahoma, Texas

6. Missouri, Arkansas, Oklahoma, Texas, New Mexico, Arizona, California

7. Arkansas, Colorado, Iowa, Kansas, Louisiana, Minnesota, Missouri, Montana, Nebraska, North Dakota, Oklahoma, South Dakota, Wyoming

8. Arizona, California, Colorado, Nevada, New Mexico, Utah, Wyoming

9. Idaho, Montana, Oregon, Washington, Wyoming

10. Connecticut, Massachusetts, New Jersey, New York, Pennsylvania

11. New York, Pennsylvania, Ohio, Michigan, Wisconsin, Minnesota, North Dakota

12. a. Maine – Georgia
    b. Washington – California
    c. Montana – New Mexico

13. Vermont

14. Nevada

15. Alabama, Arkansas, Florida, Georgia, Louisiana, Mississippi, North Carolina, South Carolina, Tennessee, Texas, Virginia

16. Connecticut, Maine, Massachusetts, New Hampshire, Rhode Island, Vermont

17. Missouri, Kansas, Nebraska, Wyoming, Idaho, Oregon (sometimes Washington is counted)

18. Idaho and Wyoming

19. Missouri, Kansas, Iowa, Nebraska, South Dakota, North Dakota, Montana, Idaho, Washington, Oregon (some include Camp Wood in Illinois)

20. Oregon

21. Idaho

22. Wyoming

23. Illinois, Missouri, Kansas, Oklahoma, Texas, New Mexico, Arizona, California

24. Missouri, Kansas, Colorado, Oklahoma, New Mexico

25. Connecticut, Delaware, Georgia, Maryland, Massachusetts, New Hampshire, New Jersey, New York, North Carolina, Pennsylvania, Rhode Island, South Carolina, Virginia

26. a. Missouri – New Mexico
    b. Texas – Kansas
    c. Missouri – Oregon
    d. Missouri – California
    e. Missouri – California
    f. Mississippi – Tennessee
    g. Illinois – Utah
    h. Wyoming – Montana
    i. Wyoming – South Dakota
    j Montana – Oregon

27. Arizona and New Mexico

28. Oklahoma

29. a. North and South Carolina
    b. New Mexico and Texas
    c. Montana and Wyoming
    d. California and Oregon
    e. Kansas and Nebraska
    f. Michigan
    g. Wisconsin
    h. New York

30. Alaska, Idaho, Nevada, Utah

31. Nevada

32. New Hampshire, New Jersey, New Mexico, New York, North Carolina, North Dakota, Rhode Island, South Carolina, South Dakota, West Virginia

33. Alabama, Alaska, Arizona, Ohio

34. Maine, Maryland, Massachusetts, Michigan, Minnesota, Mississippi, Missouri, Montana

35. Nebraska, Nevada, New Hampshire, New Jersey, New Mexico, New York, North Carolina, North Dakota

36. a. Georgia, Minnesota, Montana, Nevada

    b. Ohio, Alabama, Arizona, Oregon

    c. Florida, Texas, New Mexico, California

37. a. South Dakota, Iowa, Kansas, Wyoming

    b. Wisconsin, West Virginia, Arkansas, Utah

    c. Minnesota, Maine, Maryland, Nebraska

    d. Wyoming, Missouri, Texas, Arizona

    e. Vermont, Massachusetts, Delaware, Pennsylvania

38. 0 – (7) Rhode Island
    1 – (6) Pennsylvania
    2 – (8) South Carolina
    3 – (9) Tennessee
    4 – (3) Michigan
    5 – (4) Montana
    6 – (1) Illinois
    7 – (2) Louisiana
    8 – (5) Nevada
    9 – (10) Washington

39. a. New Mexico
    b. Montana
    c. Nebraska
    d. Indiana
    e. Alabama
    f. West Virginia

40. a. Georgia
    b. North Carolina
    c. Mississippi
    d. Nebraska
    e. Colorado
    f. North Dakota

41. Part I: a. (6) Virginia
             b. (4) North Carolina
             c. (3) Minnesota
             d. (1) Iowa
             e. (2) Louisiana
             f. (5) Oklahoma

    Part II: a. (3) Montana
             b. (5) Oregon
             c. (1) Alaska
             d. (6) Washington
             e. (2) Arizona
             f. (4) New Jersey

    Part III: a. (6) Virginia
             b. (1) California
             c. (4) Nevada
             d. (3) Idaho
             e. (2) Colorado
             f. (5) Texas

42. Part I: a. (2) California
             b. (4) Oregon
             c. (6) Washington
             d. (3) New Mexico
             e. (5) Texas
             f. (1) Alabama

Part II: a. (6) Wisconsin
          b. (4) New Hampshire
          c. (2) Minnesota
          d. (3) Nebraska
          e. (1) Colorado
          f. (5) Utah

Part III: a. (6) Wyoming
          b. (4) Montana
          c. (1) Idaho
          d. (3) Michigan
          e. (2) Indiana
          f. (5) Nevada

43. Part I: a. (2) Missouri
             b. (3) Nevada
             c. (7) Texas
             d. (4) Oregon
             e. (5) Pennsylvania
             f. (1) California
             g. (6) South Carolina
             h. (8) Washington

    Part II: a. (3) Minnesota
              b. (5) New Mexico
              c. (7) Utah
              d. (4) Montana
              e. (1) Alaska
              f. (2) Arizona
              g. (6) North Carolina
              h. (8) Wisconsin

Part III: a. (7) Ohio
          b. (4) Illinois
          c. (2) Arkansas
          d. (8) Tennessee
          e. (1) Alabama
          f. (6) Mississippi
          g. (5) Louisiana
          h. (3) Idaho

44. Illinois, Indiana, Kentucky, Ohio, West Virginia

45. Alabama, Florida, Georgia, Louisiana, Mississippi, South Carolina, Texas

46. Alabama, Georgia, Louisiana, North Carolina, South Carolina, Virginia

47. Ohio, Illinois, Indiana, Michigan, Wisconsin

48. Arizona, Colorado, Idaho, Montana, Nevada, New Mexico, Utah, Wyoming

49. Arkansas, Georgia, Kentucky, North Carolina, South Carolina, Tennessee, West Virginia

50. Arizona, California, Colorado, Idaho, Montana, Nevada, New Mexico, Oregon, Utah, Washington, Wyoming

MONUMENTS, MEMORIALS AND MUSEUMS

1. What state has the greatest number of U.S. Park Service National Monuments?

2. Where is the tallest monument in the United States?

3. Our first National Monument is in what state?

4. The tallest column in the United States is in what state?

5. Mt. Rushmore is in what state?

6. In what states are the following National Memorials?

   a. Chamizal
   b. Coronado
   c. De Soto
   d. Lincoln Boyhood
   e. Perry's Victory and International Peace Memorial
   f. Thaddeus Kosciuszko
   g. Arlington House
   h. General Grant

   (1) Arizona
   (2) Florida
   (3) Indiana
   (4) Ohio
   (5) Pennsylvania
   (6) New York
   (7) Texas
   (8) Virginia

7. In what states are the following art museums?

   Part I:
   a. Spencer Museum of Art
   b. Frederic Remington Art Museum
   c. The Nelson-Atkins Museum of Art
   d. Philbrook Museum of Art
   e. J. Paul Getty Museum
   f. Gibbes Museum of Art

   (1) California (Malibu)
   (2) Kansas (Lawrence)
   (3) New York (Ogdensburg)
   (4) Missouri (Kansas City)
   (5) Oklahoma (Tulsa)
   (6) South Carolina (Charleston)

   Part II:
   a. The Ringling Museum of Art
   b. C. M. Russell Museum
   c. Joslyn Art Museum
   d. M. H. de Young Memorial Museum
   e. Museum of International Folk Art
   f. The Cloisters

   (1) California (San Francisco)
   (2) Florida (Sarasota)
   (3) Montana (Great Falls)
   (4) Nebraska (Omaha)
   (5) New Mexico (Santa Fe)
   (6) New York (New York City)

8. In what states are the following memorials?

    a. Tomb of the Unknown Soldier
    b. Paul Bunyan Blue Ox
    c. Jefferson National Expansion Memorial N.H.S.
    d. Wright Brothers National Memorial
    e. Crazy Horse Memorial
    f. Sgt. Charles Floyd Memorial
    g. Minute Man Statue
    h. Brigham Young Statue
    i. Booker T. Washington Monument

    (1) Alabama
    (2) Iowa
    (3) Massachusetts
    (4) Minnesota
    (5) Missouri
    (6) North Carolina
    (7) South Dakota
    (8) Utah
    (9) Virginia

9. In what states are the following unusual museums?

    a. Uncle Remus Museum
    b. John Dillinger Historical Museum
    c. Bullfight Museum
    d. Tom Mix Museum
    e. Lum 'N Abner Museum
    f. Dizzy Dean Museum
    g. The Edgar Allan Poe Museum
    h. Nut Museum
    i. Cookie Jar Museum
    j. Barbed Wire Museum
    k. Liberace Museum
    l. The Old Slave Mart Museum

    (1) Arkansas (Pine Ridge)
    (2) Connecticut (Old Lyme)
    (3) Georgia (Eatonton)
    (4) Illinois (Lemont)
    (5) Indiana (Nashville)
    (6) Kansas (La Crosse)
    (7) Mississippi (Jackson)
    (8) Nevada (Las Vegas)
    (9) Oklahoma (Dewey)
    (10) South Carolina (Sullivan's Island)
    (11) Texas (El Paso)
    (12) Virginia (Richmond)

10. In what states are the following historic mills?

    a. Newlin Grist Mill
    b. Neligh Mills
    c. War Eagle Mill
    d. Old Wye Mill
    e. Tuthill Town Grist Mill
    f. Thomas Kay Woolen Mill
    g. Gaston's Mill

    (1) Arkansas (Rogers)
    (2) Maryland
    (3) Nebraska
    (4) New York (Gardiner)
    (5) Ohio (East Liverpool)
    (6) Oregon (Salem)
    (7) Pennsylvania (Glen Mills)

11. In what states are the following museums?

    Part I:
    a. Franklin Institute Science Museum
    b. Museum of Appalachia
    c. Ships of the Sea Maritime Museum
    d. Solomon R. Guggenheim Museum
    e. B&O Railroad Museum
    f. Museum of Science and Industry
    g. Carver Museum
    h. Witte Museum
    i. Museum of the Rockies

    (1) Alabama (Tuskegee)
    (2) Georgia (Savannah)
    (3) Illinois (Chicago)
    (4) Maryland (Baltimore)
    (5) Montana (Bozeman)
    (6) New York (New York City)
    (7) Pennsylvania (Philadelphia)
    (8) Tennessee (Norris)
    (9) Texas (San Antonio)

    Part II:
    a. Strawberry Banke Museum
    b. Shelburne Museum
    c. Call of the Wild Museum
    d. Stuhr Museum of the Prairie Pioneer
    e. Rosicrucian Egyptian Museum
    f. Buffalo Bill Historical Center
    g. Smoki Museum
    h. Hagley Museum
    i. Ruthmere Museum

    (1) Arizona (Prescott)
    (2) California (San Jose)
    (3) Delaware (Wilmington)
    (4) Indiana (Elkhart)
    (5) Michigan (Gaylord)
    (6) Nebraska (Grand Island)
    (7) New Hampshire (Portsmouth)
    (8) Vermont
    (9) Wyoming

12. In what states are the following farm and living history museums?

    Part I:
    a. Old Sturbridge Village
    b. Oliver H. Kelley Farm
    c. Century Village
    d. Hickory Ridge Homestead
    e. Ronald V. Jensen Living Historical Farm
    f. Living History Farms

    (1) Iowa
    (2) Massachusetts
    (3) Minnesota
    (4) North Carolina
    (5) Ohio
    (6) Utah

    Part II:
    a. Norlands Living History Center
    b. Buckley Homestead
    c. Florewood River Plantation
    d. The Homeplace – 1850
    e. Cobblestone Farm
    f. Allaire Village, Inc.

    (1) Indiana
    (2) Kentucky
    (3) Maine
    (4) Michigan
    (5) Mississippi
    (6) New Jersey

13. In what states are the following National Monuments?

Part I:

a. Ocmulgee	(1) Alaska
b. Agate Fossil Beds	(2) Arizona
c. Effigy Mounds	(3) California
d. Fossil Butte	(4) Colorado
e. Admiralty Island	(5) Georgia
f. Devil's Postpile	(6) Iowa
g. Bandelier	(7) Nebraska
h. Castle Clinton	(8) New Mexico
i. Cedar Breaks	(9) New York
j. Black Canyon of the Gunnison	(10) Utah
k. Walnut Canyon	(11) Virginia
l. George Washington Birthplace	(12) Wyoming

Part II:

a. Capulin Mountain	(1) Alabama
b. Lava Beds	(2) Alaska
c. Timpanogos Cave	(3) Arizona
d. Jewel Cave	(4) California
e. Great Sand Dunes	(5) Colorado
f. Pipe Springs	(6) Florida
g. Misty Fjords	(7) Minnesota
h. Russell Cave	(8) Nebraska
i. Mound City Group	(9) New Mexico
j. Homestead	(10) Ohio
k. Pipestone	(11) South Dakota
l. Castillo De San Marcos	(12) Utah

Part III:

a. Aztec Ruins	(1) Arizona
b. Cabrillo	(2) California
c. Congaree Swamp	(3) Colorado
d. Florissant Fossil Beds	(4) Idaho
e. George Washington Carver	(5) Louisiana
f. Grand Portage	(6) New Mexico
g. Hagerman Fossil Beds	(7) Minnesota
h. John Day Fossil Beds	(8) Missouri
i. Montezuma Castle	(9) Nebraska
j. Natural Bridges	(10) Oregon
k. Scotts Bluff	(11) South Carolina
l. Poverty Point	(12) Utah

ANSWERS TO
MONUMENTS, MEMORIALS AND MUSEUMS

1. Arizona

2. Missouri (the Gateway Arch, St. Louis – 630 feet)

3. Wyoming (Devils Tower)

4. Texas (commemorates the Battle of San Jacinto – 570 feet)

5. South Dakota

6. a. (7) Texas
   b. (1) Arizona
   c. (2) Florida
   d. (3) Indiana
   e. (4) Ohio
   f. (5) Pennsylvania
   g. (8) Virginia
   h. (6) New York

7. Part I: a. (2) Kansas
            b. (3) New York
            c. (4) Missouri
            d. (5) Oklahoma
            e. (1) California
            f. (6) South Carolina

   Part II: a. (2) Florida
            b. (3) Montana
            c. (4) Nebraska
            d. (1) California
            e. (5) New Mexico
            f. (6) New York

8. a. (9) Virginia
   b. (4) Minnesota
   c. (5) Missouri
   d. (6) North Carolina
   e. (7) South Dakota
   f. (2) Iowa
   g. (3) Massachusetts
   h. (8) Utah
   i. (1) Alabama

9. a. (3) Georgia
   b. (5) Indiana
   c. (11) Texas
   d. (9) Oklahoma
   e. (1) Arkansas
   f. (7) Mississippi
   g. (12) Virginia
   h. (2) Connecticut
   i. (4) Illinois
   j. (6) Kansas
   k. (8) Nevada
   l. (10) South Carolina

10. a. (7) Pennsylvania
    b. (3) Nebraska
    c. (1) Arkansas
    d. (2) Maryland
    e. (4) New York
    f. (6) Oregon
    g. (5) Ohio

11. Part I: a. (7) Pennsylvania
             b. (8) Tennessee
             c. (2) Georgia
             d. (6) New York
             e. (4) Maryland
             f. (3) Illinois
             g. (1) Alabama
             h. (9) Texas
             i. (5) Montana

    Part II: a. (7) New Hampshire
             b. (8) Vermont
             c. (5) Michigan
             d. (6) Nebraska
             e. (2) California
             f. (9) Wyoming
             g. (1) Arizona
             h. (3) Delaware
             i. (4) Indiana

12. Part I: a. (2) Massachusetts
             b. (3) Minnesota
             c. (5) Ohio
             d. (4) North Carolina
             e. (6) Utah
             f. (1) Iowa

Part II: a. (3) Maine
              b. (1) Indiana
              c. (5) Mississippi
              d. (2) Kentucky
              e. (4) Michigan
              f. (6) New Jersey

13. Part I: a. (5) Georgia
              b. (7) Nebraska
              c. (6) Iowa
              d. (12) Wyoming
              e. (1) Alaska
              f. (3) California
              g. (8) New Mexico
              h. (9) New York
              i. (10) Utah
              j. (4) Colorado
              k. (2) Arizona
              l. (11) Virginia

Part II: a. (9) New Mexico
              b. (4) California
              c. (12) Utah
              d. (11) South Dakota
              e. (5) Colorado
              f. (3) Arizona
              g. (2) Alaska
              h. (1) Alabama
              i. (10) Ohio
              j. (8) Nebraska
              k. (7) Minnesota
              l. (6) Florida

Part III: a. (6) New Mexico
              b. (2) California
              c. (11) South Carolina
              d. (3) Colorado
              e. (8) Missouri
              f. (7) Minnesota
              g. (4) Idaho
              h. (10) Oregon
              i. (1) Arizona
              j. (12) Utah
              k. (9) Nebraska
              l. (5) Louisiana

NATURE AND NAMES

1. Name the four states which are commonwealths.

2. This state started its colonial history under Dutch rule as New Amsterdam. Name it.

3. What state's soldiers during the civil war complained that the men from North Carolina didn't hold their positions—that is, they didn't put "tar on their heels?"

4. With which state is the word Deseret associated?

5. Among the 48 contiguous states, which states name was the only one about which pronunciation and spelling ever rose to be a major issue?

6. Montana had been suggested by Congress as a territory name for what current state?

7. The name Idaho failed by only the narrowest of margins to be applied to what state name (territory) by Congress?

8. A territory which eventually became a state originally was know as Washoe. What state is it?

9. The passion flower is the official state wild flower of what state?

10. What state is named after a President?

11. Which state was known as Indian Territory?

12. In what state was the first national bird sanctuary?

13. What states were named for England's Charles I?

14. What state is named after a valley in Pennsylvania?

15. What state bears the name of a county in England?

16. What is the only state name that ends with an "h"?

17. Name the state whose inhabitants are known as freemen?

18. What state was called the dark and bloody ground because it was the scene of frequent Indian wars?

19. A United States battleship named after a state was destroyed by an explosion in Havana Harbor in 1898. Name the state.

20. Which state was originally called the Province of Laconia?

21. The highest temperature ever recorded in the United States was in what state?

22. The lowest temperature ever recorded in the United States was in what state?

23. The world's record of the highest surface wind speed took place in which state?

24. The so-called independent State of Franklin was made up of parts of which two states.

25. In 1941, a movement to create the State of Jefferson was making progress until December 7th. Portions of which two states were to be included in this new state?

26. Three states are sometimes called the sunshine state. Name them.

27. Two states are sometimes called the silver state. Name them.

28. Two states are sometimes called the beaver state. Name them.

29. What state has the longest official name?

30. Due to the number of battles and skirmishes, which state became known as the "Pathway of the Revolution?"

31. What is the only state where the state flower is the blossom of the state tree?

32. What state is the only one with a name of one syllable?

33. Fort Van Buren was established in 1835 by the American Fur Company and named for the President. In what future state was it in?

34. What current state was originally named after the Earl of Sandwich?

35. What state is named after a country?

36. What state is sometimes considered to be associated by name to a French province (not 100% proven)?

37. What state is named after an island?

38. There are at least ten states named after a person or some aspect of that person. Name them.

39. Which state has more national champion trees then any other?

40. Which state has more life zones than any other?

41. The label "Country Music Capital" relates to a city in what state?

42. What state contains a lake which has a name that is the longest word in the English language?

43. Which two states names end in double letters?

44. Which two states have official beverages of tomato juice and cranberry juice?

45. The bolo tie is the official neckware of which state?

46. The following is a list of state insects. Match the state to the insect.

    a. Firefly

    b. Monarch butterfly

    c. Praying mantis

47. The bizcochito is the official cookie of which state?

48. The blue crab is what state's official crustacean?

49. The Scotch bonnet is the official state shell of which state?

50. The mammoth is the official state fossil of which state?

51. The oyster shell is the official shell of which state?

52. The chile and frijol are the official state vegetables of which state?

53. The last name of a President is listed. The number following the name represents the number of states where a fort, blockhouse, barrack, camp, cantonment, battery, or station with the President's name is or has been located. Try to name at least half the states.
    a. Jefferson (five)
    b. Madison (nine)
    c. Monroe (four)
    d. Lincoln (fourteen)
    e. Tyler (seven)
    f. Polk (four)

54. The following is a list of state birds. Match the state to the bird.

    Part I:
a. Willow ptarmigan	(1) Alaska
b. Brown thrasher	(2) Georgia
c. Purple finch	(3) Minnesota
d. Common loon	(4) New Hampshire
e. Roadrunner	(5) New Mexico
f. Scissor-tailed flycatcher	(6) Oklahoma

Part II:

a. Ruffed grouse
b. Seagull
c. Hermit thrush
d. Ring-necked pheasant
e. Willow goldfinch

(1) Pennsylvania
(2) South Dakota
(3) Utah
(4) Vermont
(5) Washington

55. The following is a list of official state animals. Match the state to the animal.

a. Sperm whale
b. Rocky Mountain bighorn sheep
c. Desert bighorn sheep
d. Coyote
e. Grizzly bear
f. Raccoon
g. Badger
h. Gray squirrel

(1) California
(2) Colorado
(3) Connecticut
(4) Nevada
(5) North Carolina
(6) South Dakota
(7) Tennessee
(8) Wisconsin

56. The following is a list of official state flowers. Match the state to the flower.

Part I:

a. Black-eyed Susan
b. Mountain laurel
c. Sego lily
d. Cherokee rose
e. Peach blossom
f. Hawthorn
g. Mistletoe
h. Violet
i. Dogwood
j. Bitterroot
k. Orange blossom

(1) Delaware
(2) Florida
(3) Georgia
(4) Maryland
(5) Missouri
(6) Montana
(7) North Carolina
(8) Oklahoma
(9) Pennsylvania
(10) Rhode Island
(11) Utah

Part II:

a. Sunflower	(1) California
b. Indian paintbrush	(2) Hawaii
c. Iris	(3) Indiana
d. Golden poppy	(4) Kansas
e. Tulip	(5) Michigan
f. Orchid	(6) Nevada
g. Yellow jasmine	(7) South Carolina
h. Bluebonnet	(8) Tennessee
i. Red clover	(9) Texas
j. Sagebrush	(10) Vermont
k. Apple blossom	(11) Wyoming

57. The following is a list of official state fish. Match the state to the fish.

a. Musky	(1) Alaska
b. Chinook salmon	(2) California
c. Cutthroat trout	(3) Maine
d. Landlocked salmon	(4) Maryland
e. Rockfish	(5) New Mexico
f. King salmon	(6) Oregon
g. Golden trout	(7) Wisconsin

58. The following is a list of official state trees. Match the state to the tree.

Part I:

a. Tuliptree	(1) Delaware
b. American holly	(2) Indiana
c. White birch	(3) Kentucky
d. Coffeetree	(4) Mississippi
e. Magnolia	(5) Montana
f. Ponderosa pine	(6) New Hampshire
g. Red oak	(7) New Jersey

Part II:

a. Western hemlock	(1) Alaska
b. Redbud	(2) Hawaii
c. Palmetto	(3) Ohio
d. Pecan	(4) Oklahoma
e. Blue spruce	(5) South Carolina
f. Sitka spruce	(6) Texas
g. Candlenut	(7) Utah
h. Buckeye	(8) Washington

59. In what states are found the following famous trees?

   Part I:
   a. Evangeline Oak
   b. Post Office Oak
   c. Joyce Kilmer Tree
   d. Daniel Boone's "BAR" Tree
   e. Charter Oak

   (1) Connecticut (Hartford)
   (2) Kansas (Council Grove)
   (3) Louisiana (St. Martinsville)
   (4) New Jersey (New Brunswick)
   (5) Tennessee

   Part II:
   a. Quaker Meeting House Tree
   b. General Fremont Tree
   c. Jail Tree
   d. Mullan Tree
   e. God's Tree

   (1) Arizona (Wickenberg)
   (2) California
   (3) Idaho
   (4) New York (Flushing)
   (5) Texas (La Feria)

60. The following National Champion trees are located in which states? (Species are determined by total mass of each tree.)

   Part I:
   a. American beech
   b. American elder
   c. Tamarisk
   d. Sassafras
   e. Pecan
   f. Mango

   (1) Florida
   (2) Kentucky
   (3) New Mexico
   (4) Ohio
   (5) Tennessee
   (6) Virginia

   Part II:
   a. Mountain laurel
   b. Nannyberry
   c. Bitter cherry
   d. American elm
   e. Sierra bladdernut
   f. Gray birch

   (1) California
   (2) Connecticut
   (3) Kansas
   (4) Michigan
   (5) North Carolina
   (6) Washington

61. In what states are the following Aquariums?

   Part I:
   a. Steinhart Aquarium
   b. Mystic Marinelife Aquarium
   c. Ak-Sar-Ben Aquarium
   d. Mount Desert Oceanarium
   e. Mote Marine Science Aquarium

   (1) California (San Francisco)
   (2) Connecticut
   (3) Florida (Sarasota)
   (4) Maine (Southwest Harbor)
   (5) Nebraska (Gretna)

Part II:
  a. Aquarium of the Americas
  b. Kipp Aquarium
  c. John G. Shedd Aquarium
  d. Belle Isle Aquarium
  e. Depoe Bay Aquarium

(1) Illinois (Chicago)
(2) Louisiana (New Orleans)
(3) Michigan (Detroit)
(4) Oregon
(5) Texas (Houston)

62. In what states are the following gardens?

Part I:
  a. Moorten Botanical Garden
  b. Elitch Gardens
  c. Longwood Gardens
  d. Callaway Gardens
  e. Hampton-Preston Mansion and Garden
  f. Kingwood Center

(1) California (Palm Springs)
(2) Colorado (Denver)
(3) Georgia (Pine Mountain)
(4) Ohio (Mansfield)
(5) Pennsylvania
(6) South Carolina (Columbia)

Part II:
  a. Longwood Gardens
  b. Bellingrath Gardens and Home
  c. Maclay State Gardens
  d. Boyce Thompson Southwestern Arboretum
  e. The Elms
  f. Sonnenberg Gardens

(1) Alabama (Theodore)
(2) Arizona (Superior)
(3) Delaware (Wilmington)
(4) Florida (Tallahassee)
(5) New York (Canandaigua)
(6) Rhode island (Newport)

63. In what state are the following zoological parks?

Part I:
  a. Chaffee Zoological Gardens
  b. Beardsley Zoo
  c. Sedgwick County Zoo
  d. Brookfield Zoo
  e. Gladys Porter Zoo

(1) California (Fresno)
(2) Connecticut (Bridgeport)
(3) Illinois
(4) Kansas (Wichita)
(5) Texas (Brownsville)

Part II:
  a. Metro Washington Park Zoo
  b. Metrozoo
  c. Burnett Park Zoo
  d. Great Plains Zoo
  e. Oglebay's Good Children's Zoo

(1) Florida (Miami-Miami Beach)
(2) New York (Syracuse)
(3) Oregon (Portland)
(4) South Dakota (Sioux Falls)
(5) West Virginia (Wheeling)

64. The following are state mottoes. Name the state they represent.

Part I:
a. Union, justice and confidence
b. Under God the people rule
c. With God, all things are possible
d. God enriches (Ditat Deus)
e. By valor and arms (Virtute et armis)
f. The people rule (Regnat populus)

(1) Arizona
(2) Arkansas
(3) Louisiana
(4) Mississippi
(5) Ohio
(6) South Dakota

Part II:
a. Wisdom, justice and moderation
b. It grows as it goes (Crescit eundo)
c. Equality before the law
d. Virtue, liberty and independence
e. United we stand, divided we fall
f. All for our country

(1) Georgia
(2) Kentucky
(3) Nebraska
(4) Nevada
(5) New Mexico
(6) Pennsylvania

Part III:
a. Live free or die
b. Eureka (I have found it)
c. Industry
d. Hope
e. Forward
f. Friendship

(1) California
(2) New Hampshire
(3) Rhode Island
(4) Texas
(5) Utah
(6) Wisconsin

Part IV:
a. The Union
b. Freedom and unity
c. Agriculture, commerce
d. Liberty and prosperity
e. Liberty and independence
f. In God we trust

(1) Delaware
(2) Florida
(3) New Jersey
(4) Oregon
(5) Tennessee
(6) Vermont

65. Match the states to the names or descriptive term indicating its name origin.

Part I:
a. Indian "Great Lake"
b. Indian "Beside the long tidal river"
c. Indian "Sky-tinted water"
d. Indian "Tribe of superior men"
e. Indian "I clear the thicket"
f. Indian "Friends"
g. Indian "Place of the little springs"
h. Indian "People of the south wind"

(1) Alabama
(2) Arizona
(3) Connecticut
(4) Illinois
(5) Kansas
(6) Michigan
(7) Minnesota
(8) Texas

Part II:

a.	Indian "Land of tomorrow"	(1)	Alaska
b.	Indian "Mountains and valleys alternating"	(2)	Florida
c.	Indian "Father of waters"	(3)	Kentucky
d.	Indian "People of the big canoes"	(4)	Mississippi
e.	Aleut "Great land"	(5)	Missouri
f.	Spanish "Feast of flowers"	(6)	Ohio
g.	Indian "Great river"	(7)	Utah
h.	Indian "People of the mountains"	(8)	Wyoming

Part III:

a.	Spanish "Red"	(1)	Colorado
b.	Indian "Great mountain place"	(2)	Iowa
c.	Indian "River in the flatness"	(3)	Massachusetts
d.	French "Green mountain"	(4)	Nebraska
e.	Indian "Gathering of waters"	(5)	Nevada
f.	Indian "This is the place"	(6)	Oklahoma
g.	Spanish "Snow-clad"	(7)	Vermont
h.	Indian "Red People"	(8)	Wisconsin

66. The following are nicknames of state universities and colleges. Name the state.

Part I:

a.	Blue Hens	(1)	Delaware
b.	Black Bears	(2)	Georgia
c.	Bulldogs	(3)	Kentucky
d.	Mountaineers	(4)	Maine
e.	Cowboys	(5)	Montana
f.	Grizzlies	(6)	New York
g.	Violets	(7)	North Carolina
h.	Wildcats	(8)	Pennsylvania
i.	Quakers	(9)	West Virginia
j.	Tar Heels	(10)	Wyoming

Part II:

a.	Gamecocks	(1)	Alabama
b.	Catamounts	(2)	California
c.	Rams	(3)	Florida
d.	Rebels	(4)	Minnesota
e.	Utes	(5)	Mississippi
f.	Gators	(6)	Nebraska
g.	Crimson Tide	(7)	Rhode Island
h.	Golden Bears	(8)	South Carolina
i.	Gophers	(9)	Utah
j.	Cornhuskers	(10)	Vermont

Part III:

a. Jayhawks	(1) Arkansas
b. Longhorns	(2) Colorado
c. Redmen	(3) Illinois
d. Razorbacks	(4) Kansas
e. Terrapins	(5) Maryland
f. Fighting Illini	(6) Massachusetts
g. Buffaloes	(7) Missouri
h. Ducks (Webfoots)	(8) Oregon
i. Cavaliers	(9) Texas
j. Tigers	(10) Virginia

67. The following nicknames relate to which states?

Part I:

a. Granite State	(1) Connecticut
b. Palmetto State	(2) Mississippi
c. Garden State	(3) Nebraska
d. Empire State	(4) New Hampshire
e. Green Mountain State	(5) New Jersey
f. Beef State	(6) New York
g. Magnolia State	(7) South Carolina
h. Lone Star State	(8) Texas
i. The Old Dominion	(9) Vermont
j. Constitution State	(10) Virginia

Part II:

a. Diamond State	(1) Alabama
b. Cactus State	(2) Arizona
c. North Star State	(3) Connecticut
d. Sioux State	(4) Delaware
e. Prairie State	(5) Georgia
f. Nutmeg State	(6) Illinois
g. Sunset State	(7) Minnesota
h. Yellowhammer State	(8) New Mexico
i. Chinook State	(9) North Dakota
j. Empire State of the South	(10) Washington

Part III:

a.	Hawkeye State	(1)	Indiana
b.	Old Colony State	(2)	Iowa
c.	Sunflower State	(3)	Kansas
d.	Old North State	(4)	Louisiana
e.	Sooner State	(5)	Massachusetts
f.	Hoosier State	(6)	Nevada
g.	Volunteer State	(7)	North Carolina
h.	Little Rhody	(8)	Oklahoma
i.	Battle Born State	(9)	Rhode Island
j.	Creole State	(10)	Tennessee

Part IV:

a.	Centennial State	(1)	Arkansas
b.	Land of Opportunity	(2)	California
c.	Golden State	(3)	Colorado
d.	First State	(4)	Delaware
e.	Peach State	(5)	Georgia
f.	Buckeye State	(6)	Maryland
g.	Coyote State	(7)	Michigan
h.	Badger State	(8)	Ohio
i.	Wolverine State	(9)	South Dakota
j.	Old Line State	(10)	Wisconsin

Part V:

a.	Sugar State	(1)	Alabama
b.	Free State	(2)	Alaska
c.	Big Sky State	(3)	Arizona
d.	Tree Planters State	(4)	Arkansas
e.	Bay State	(5)	Idaho
f.	Heart of Dixie	(6)	Louisiana
g.	Wonder State	(7)	Maryland
h.	Gem of the Mountains	(8)	Massachusetts
i.	Apache State	(9)	Montana
j.	The Last Frontier	(10)	Nebraska

Part VI:

a.	Bluegrass State	(1)	Arizona
b.	Grand Canyon State	(2)	Idaho
c.	Gem State	(3)	Kentucky
d.	Pine Tree State	(4)	Maine
e.	Show-Me State	(5)	Missouri
f.	Treasure State	(6)	Montana
g.	Equality State	(7)	Pennsylvania
h.	Beehive State	(8)	Utah
i.	Keystone State	(9)	West Virginia
j.	Mountain State	(10)	Wyoming

Part VII:

a.	Land of the Midnight Sun	(1)	Alabama
b.	Cotton State	(2)	Alaska
c.	Aloha State	(3)	Hawaii
d.	Land of Lincoln	(4)	Illinois
e.	Pelican State	(5)	Louisiana
f.	Land of 10,000 Lakes	(6)	Minnesota
g.	Land of Enchantment	(7)	Nevada
h.	Flickertail State	(8)	New Mexico
i.	Evergreen State	(9)	North Dakota
j.	Sagebrush State	(10)	Washington

Part VIII:

a.	Copper State	(1)	Arizona
b.	Winter Salad Bowl State	(2)	Colorado
c.	Spud State	(3)	Florida
d.	Bean-eating State	(4)	Georgia
e.	Bread and Butter State	(5)	Idaho
f.	Goober State	(6)	Kansas
g.	Valentine State	(7)	Massachusetts
h.	Salt of the Earth	(8)	Minnesota

ANSWERS TO
NATURE AND NAMES

1. Kentucky, Massachusetts, Pennsylvania, Virginia

2. New York

3. Mississippi

4. Utah

5. Arkansas (originally Arkansaw)

6. Idaho

7. Colorado

8. Nevada

9. Tennessee

10. Washington

11. Oklahoma

12. Florida (Pelican Island was established in 1903)

13. North and South Carolina

14. Wyoming

15. New Hampshire

16. Utah

17. Vermont (referred to in the State Constitution as freemen of the State)

18. Kentucky

19. Maine

20. New Hampshire

21. California (Death Valley in 1913 – 134°F)

22. Alaska (Prospect in 1971 – -79.8°F)

23. New Hampshire (Mt. Washington – 231 MPH)

24. Tennessee and Virginia

25. California and Oregon

26. Florida, New Mexico, South Dakota

27. Colorado and Nevada

28. New York and Oregon

29. Rhode Island (State of Rhode Island and Providence Plantations)

30. New Jersey

31. Mississippi (Magnolia)

32. Maine

33. Montana (present Custer County – burned in 1842)

34. Hawaii

35. New Mexico

36. Maine (French province of Mayne)

37. New Jersey (Isle of Jersey in the English Channel)

38. Delaware, Georgia, Louisiana, Maryland, North Carolina, Pennsylvania, South Carolina, Virginia, Washington, West Virginia

39. Florida

40. California (six)

41. Tennessee (Nashville)

42. Massachusetts (Chaubunagungamaug or Lake Webster – or the Indian form Chargoggagoggmanchaugagoggchaubunagungamaug or Chargoggargoggagoggmanchuaggagoggchubunagungamaugg)

43. Hawaii and Tennessee

44. Ohio and Massachusetts

45. Arizona

46. a. Pennsylvania
    b. Illinois
    c. Connecticut

47. New Mexico

48. Maryland

49. North Carolina

50. Nebraska

51. Virginia

52. New Mexico

53. a. Florida, Illinois, Kentucky,
       Missouri, Ohio
    b. Alabama, Florida, Iowa,
       Kentucky, Maryland, Maine,
       Missouri, Mississippi,
       New York
    c. California, Florida, Ohio,
       Virginia
    d. Alabama, Arizona,
       California, Colorado,
       Florida, Iowa, Illinois,
       Kansas, Maine, Minnesota,
       North Dakota, New Jersey,
       Oregon, Texas
    e. Alabama, Colorado, Georgia,
       Illinois, New York, Ohio
       Kentucky
    f. Louisiana, North Carolina,
       Oregon, Texas

54. Part I: a. (1) Alaska
              b. (2) Georgia
              c. (4) New Hampshire
              d. (3) Minnesota
              e. (5) New Mexico
              f. (6) Oklahoma

    Part II: a. (1) Pennsylvania
              b. (3) Utah
              c. (4) Vermont
              d. (2) South Dakota
              e. (5) Washington

55. a. (3) Connecticut
    b. (2) Colorado
    c. (4) Nevada
    d. (6) South Dakota
    e. (1) California
    f. (7) Tennessee
    g. (8) Wisconsin
    h. (5) North Carolina

56. Part I: a. (4) Maryland
              b. (9) Pennsylvania
              c. (11) Utah
              d. (3) Georgia
              e. (1) Delaware
              f. (5) Missouri
              g. (8) Oklahoma
              h. (10) Rhode Island
              i. (7) North Carolina
              j. (6) Montana
              k. (2) Florida

    Part II: a. (4) Kansas
              b. (11) Wyoming
              c. (8) Tennessee
              d. (1) California
              e. (3) Indiana
              f. (2) Hawaii
              g. (7) South Carolina
              h. (9) Texas
              i. (10) Vermont
              j. (6) Nevada
              k. (5) Michigan

57. a. (7) Wisconsin
    b. (6) Oregon
    c. (5) New Mexico
    d. (3) Maine
    e. (4) Maryland
    f. (1) Alaska
    g. (2) California

58. Part I: a. (2) Indiana
              b. (1) Delaware
              c. (6) New Hampshire
              d. (3) Kentucky
              e. (4) Mississippi
              f. (5) Montana
              g. (7) New Jersey

Part II: a. (8) Washington
b. (4) Oklahoma
c. (5) South Carolina
d. (6) Texas
e. (7) Utah
f. (1) Alaska
g. (2) Hawaii
h. (3) Ohio

59. Part I: a. (3) Louisiana
b. (2) Kansas
c. (4) New Jersey
d. (5) Tennessee
e. (1) Connecticut

Part II: a. (4) New York
b. (2) California
c. (1) Arizona
d. (3) Idaho
e. (5) Texas

60. Part I: a. (4) Ohio
b. (6) Virginia
c. (3) New Mexico
d. (2) Kentucky
e. (5) Tennessee
f. (1) Florida

Part II: a. (5) North Carolina
b. (4) Michigan
c. (6) Washington
d. (3) Kansas
e. (1) California
f. (2) Connecticut

61. Part I: a. (1) California
b. (2) Connecticut
c. (5) Nebraska
d. (4) Maine
e. (3) Florida

Part II: a. (2) Louisiana
b. (5) Texas
c. (1) Illinois
d. (3) Michigan
e. (4) Oregon

62. Part I: a. (1) California
b. (2) Colorado
c. (5) Pennsylvania
d. (3) Georgia
e. (6) South Carolina
f. (4) Ohio

Part II: a. (3) Delaware
b. (1) Alabama
c. (4) Florida
d. (2) Arizona
e. (6) Rhode Island
f. (5) New York

63. Part I: a. (1) California
b. (2) Connecticut
c. (4) Kansas
d. (3) Illinois
e. (5) Texas

Part II: a. (3) Oregon
b. (1) Florida
c. (2) New York
d. (4) South Dakota
e. (5) West Virginia

64. Part I: a. (3) Louisiana
b. (6) South Dakota
c. (5) Ohio
d. (1) Arizona
e. (4) Mississippi
f. (2) Arkansas

Part II: a. (1) Georgia
b. (5) New Mexico
c. (3) Nebraska
d. (6) Pennsylvania
e. (2) Kentucky
f. (4) Nevada

Part III: a. (2) New Hampshire
b. (1) California
c. (5) Utah
d. (3) Rhode Island
e. (6) Wisconsin
f. (4) Texas

Part IV: a. (4) Oregon
b. (6) Vermont
c. (5) Tennessee
d. (3) New Jersey
e. (1) Delaware
f. (2) Florida

65. Part I: a. (6) Michigan
b. (3) Connecticut
c. (7) Minnesota
d. (4) Illinois
e. (1) Alabama
f. (8) Texas
g. (2) Arizona
h. (5) Kansas

Part II: a. (3) Kentucky
b. (8) Wyoming
c. (4) Mississippi
d. (5) Missouri
e. (1) Alaska
f. (2) Florida
g. (6) Ohio
h. (7) Utah

Part III: a. (1) Colorado
b. (3) Massachusetts
c. (4) Nebraska
d. (7) Vermont
e. (8) Wisconsin
f. (2) Iowa
g. (5) Nevada
h. (6) Oklahoma

66. Part I: a. (1) Delaware
b. (4) Maine
c. (2) Georgia
d. (9) West Virginia
e. (10) Wyoming
f. (5) Montana
g. (6) New York
h. (3) Kentucky
i. (8) Pennsylvania
j. (7) North Carolina

Part II: a. (8) South Carolina
b. (10) Vermont
c. (7) Rhode Island
d. (5) Mississippi
e. (9) Utah
f. (3) Florida
g. (1) Alabama
h. (2) California
i. (4) Minnesota
j. (6) Nebraska

Part III: a. (4) Kansas
b. (9) Texas
c. (6) Massachusetts
d. (1) Arkansas
e. (5) Maryland
f. (3) Illinois
g. (2) Colorado
h. (8) Oregon
i. (10) Virginia
j. (7) Missouri

67. Part I: a. (4) New Hampshire
b. (7) South Carolina
c. (5) New Jersey
d. (6) New York
e. (9) Vermont
f. (3) Nebraska
g. (2) Mississippi
h. (8) Texas
i. (10) Virginia
j. (1) Connecticut

Part II: a. (4) Delaware
b. (8) New Mexico
c. (7) Minnesota
d. (9) North Dakota
e. (6) Illinois
f. (3) Connecticut
g. (2) Arizona
h. (1) Alabama
i. (10) Washington
j. (5) Georgia

Part III: a. (2) Iowa
            b. (5) Massachusetts
            c. (3) Kansas
            d. (7) North Carolina
            e. (8) Oklahoma
            f. (1) Indiana
            g. (10) Tennessee
            h. (9) Rhode Island
            i. (6) Nevada
            j. (4) Louisiana

Part IV: a. (3) Colorado
            b. (1) Arkansas
            c. (2) California
            d. (4) Delaware
            e. (5) Georgia
            f. (8) Ohio
            g. (9) South Dakota
            h. (10) Wisconsin
            i. (7) Michigan
            j. (6) Maryland

Part V: a. (6) Louisiana
            b. (7) Maryland
            c. (9) Montana
            d. (10) Nebraska
            e. (8) Massachusetts
            f. (1) Alabama
            g. (4) Arkansas
            h. (5) Idaho
            i. (3) Arizona
            j. (2) Alaska

Part VI: a. (3) Kentucky
            b. (1) Arizona
            c. (2) Idaho
            d. (4) Maine
            e. (5) Missouri
            f. (6) Montana
            g. (10) Wyoming
            h. (8) Utah
            i. (7) Pennsylvania
            j. (9) West Virginia

Part VII: a. (2) Alaska
            b. (1) Alabama
            c. (3) Hawaii
            d. (4) Illinois
            e. (5) Louisiana
            f. (6) Minnesota
            g. (8) New Mexico
            h. (9) North Dakota
            i. (10) Washington
            j. (7) Nevada

Part VIII: a. (2) Colorado
            b. (3) Florida
            c. (5) Idaho
            d. (7) Massachusetts
            e. (8) Minnesota
            f. (4) Georgia
            g. (1) Arizona
            h. (6) Kansas

PEOPLE, PARKS AND PLACES

1. What is the only state that has no national parkland?

2. The largest public park in the United States is in what state?

3. In which state is the largest desert state park in the United States?

4. In what state is the world's largest chocolate factory?

5. Seward's Folly related to which state?

6. In what state is the Corn Palace?

7. In what state is London Bridge?

8. In what state is the Henry E. Huntington Library?

9. In what state is the Mayo Clinic?

10. In what state is the Going-to-the-Sun Highway?

11. In what state is supposedly the Lost Dutchman Mine?

12. Thomas Edison's laboratories were in what state?

13. Of which state was Huey Long governor when he was assassinated in 1935?

14. Hell's Canyon divides parts of which two states?

15. Okefenokee Swamp is in which two states?

16. In what state is the Valley of Ten Thousand Smokes?

17. In what state in Fire Island?

18. In what state is Walden Pond?

19. Part of three states are in the same national park. Name the states.

20. In what state is Kitty Hawk?

21. In what state is located the Tomb of the Unknown Soldier of the Confederate States of America?

22. The following United States Service Academies are located in which states?
    a. U.S. Military Academy
    b. U.S. Naval Academy
    c. U.S. Air Force Academy
    d. U.S. Coast Guard Academy
    e. U.S. Merchant Marine Academy

23. In what state is America's Stonehenge, the location of the oldest known megalithic site on the continent?

24. In what state is there a replica of the Parthenon in Athens?

25. In what state is there a replica of England's Stonehenge?

26. Reed Gold Mine State Historic Site was the first placer gold mine in the United States (1799). In what state is it found?

27. In what future state did Custer make his last stand at Little Big Horn?

28. In what state did Aaron Burr kill Alexander Hamilton in a dueling encounter?

29. During the period 1930-40, which was the fastest growing state in population?

30. Women were first given the right to vote in a western state while it was still a territory. Name the state.

31. Which four states have the largest American Indian population?

32. What state was the first to register births?

33. The largest port in the world is in which two states?

34. The world's tallest fountain is in what state?

35. Cape Cod is in which state?

36. Cape Hatteras is in which state?

37. In what state was President McKinley assassinated?

38. President Eisenhower was born in what state?

39. What was Robert E. Lee's home state?

40. The Grand Ole Opry is in which state?

41. In which state is Camp David?

42. In what state did Robert E. Lee surrender to U. S. Grant at Appomattox Courthouse?

43. What state contains the largest United States Indian Reservation?

44. Hayes, Garfield, Taft and B. Harrison were all born in what state?

45. Tyler, Taylor, Wilson and W. H. Harrison were all born in what state?

46. The governor's term of office is two years in three states. Name the states.

47. From what state did Charles Lindbergh take off in his 1927 flight to Paris in the "Spirit of St. Louis?"

48. In what state is the National Aviation Hall of Fame?

49. In what future state did Patrick Henry address a convention with his "give me liberty or give me death" speech?

50. In what state is the oldest bridge in continuous use in the United States?

51. In what future state did Dr. Marcus Whitman and Narcissa Whitman found a mission?

52. In what state was the Johnstown flood of 1889?

53. With what state is the name James E. Oglethorpe associated?

54. What was Jesse James' home state?

55. In which state was Lincoln born?

56. The Scopes trial took place in which state (William Jennings Bryan versus Clarence Darrow)?

57. To which state does Sandy Hook belong– New York or New Jersey?

58. The "Wizard of Kinderhook" was a nickname earned by President Martin Van Buren before he entered the White House in 1837. Kinderhook is in what state?

59. In John Steinbeck's "Grapes of Wrath," the Joads came from what state?

60. A national park in what state is home to bobcats, panthers, deer and manatees?

61. From what state was Jeannette Rankin, the first woman in the United States House of Representatives?

62. From what state was Hattie Carraway, the first woman United States Senator?

63. One of the passengers who escaped the sinking of the Titanic was Mrs. James J. (Molly) Brown. She became famous as "The Unsinkable Molly Brown." Her home is now a museum in what state?

64. Kitt Peak National Observatory operates the worlds largest solar telescope. What state is it in?

65. Will Rogers and Wiley Post were killed in an airplane crash in what future state?

66. In what state is the Tuskegee Institute?

67. In what state is the grave of Sgt. Charles Floyd, the only fatality of the Lewis and Clark expedition?

68. A federal prison nicknamed "The Rock" is in what state?

69. The first United States president born west of the Mississippi River was from what state?

70. The driving in of a golden spike marked the completion of the first transcontinental railroad (however, various locations had not yet been connected). In what state did this take place?

71. The Morgan horse is considered the only breed originating in the United States. Justin Morgan developed it in what state in the late 1700s?

72. In what state were eight United States presidents born?

73. In what state were seven United States presidents born?

74. In which two states were four United States presidents born?

75. In what state is the John D. Rockefeller, Jr. Parkway?

76. A Fort Union or Camp Union was located in thirteen states. Name as many as you can.

77. A Fort Davis or Camp Davis was located in eight states. Name as many as you can.

78. In what states are the following?
    a. Kennedy Space Center
    b. Johnson Space Center
    c. Jet Propulsion Laboratory
    d. Marshall Space Flight Center

79. In what states do the following festivals take place?

    a. National Basque Festival   (1) California
    b. National Date Festival   (2) Idaho
    c. National Old-Time Fiddler's   (3) Nevada
       Contest and Festival   (4) Oregon
    d. Green River Rendezvous   (5) Utah
    e. World Championship Timber   (6) Wyoming
       Carnival
    f. Golden Spike Celebration

80. In what states are or were the following communes located?

a. Fountaingrove   (1) California
b. The Oneida Community   (2) Indiana
c. The Separatists of Zoar   (3) Iowa
d. New Harmony (George Rapp   (4) Michigan
    and Robert Owen)   (5) New York
e. Ephrata Colony   (6) Ohio
f. The Amana Society   (7) Pennsylvania
g. The House of David

81. In what states are the following famous hotels?

a. Grossinger's   (1) California
b. Beverly Hills   (2) Florida
c. Halekulani   (3) Hawaii
d. Fountainebleau   (4) Illinois
e. Waldorf-Astoria   (5) Minnesota
f. Benjamin Franklin   (6) New York
g. Palmer House   (7) New York
h. Nicollet   (8) Pennsylvania

82. In what states are the following presidential libraries?

a. Herbert Hoover   (1) California
b. Jimmy Carter   (2) California
c. Harry Truman   (3) Georgia
d. Dwight Eisenhower   (4) Iowa
e. Lyndon Johnson   (5) Kansas
f. John Kennedy   (6) Massachusetts
g. Ronald Reagan   (7) Missouri
h. Richard Nixon   (8) New York
i. Franklin Roosevelt   (9) Texas

83. In what states are or were the following prisons, penal camps, jails or reformatories?

Part I: a. Andersonville Prison   (1) California
           b. Sing Sing Prison   (2) Georgia
           c. Folsom State Penitentiary   (3) Massachusetts
           d. McNeil Island Federal   (4) New York
              Prison   (5) Washington
           e. Framington Reformatory

Part II:

a. Newgate Prison
b. Chillicothe Reformatory
c. Libby Prison
d. Sandstone Correctional Institution
e. Attica Prison

(1) Connecticut
(2) Minnesota
(3) New York
(4) Ohio
(5) Virginia

84. In what states are the following Civil War Battlefields?

Part I:

a. Glorieta
b. Wilson's Creek
c. Perryville
d. The Wilderness
e. Resaca
f. Stones River

(1) Georgia
(2) Kentucky
(3) Missouri
(4) New Mexico
(5) Tennessee
(6) Virginia

Part II:

a. Brices Cross Roads
b. Harpers Ferry
c. South Mountain
d. Gettysburg
e. Honey Springs
f. Port Hudson

(1) Louisiana
(2) Maryland
(3) Mississippi
(4) Oklahoma
(5) Pennsylvania
(6) West Virginia

85. In which states are the following National Military Sites?

a. Fort Necessity
b. Guilford Courthouse
c. Pea Ridge
d. Shiloh
e. Manassas
f. Vicksburg
g. Antietam
h. Horseshoe Bend
i. Cowpens
j. Kenesaw Mountain

(1) Alabama
(2) Arkansas
(3) Georgia
(4) Maryland
(5) Mississippi
(6) North Carolina
(7) Pennsylvania
(8) South Carolina
(9) Tennessee
(10) Virginia

86. The following Park Service National Historic Sites are in which states?

   a. Theodore Roosevelt Birthplace NHS
   b. Abraham Lincoln Birthplace NHS
   c. Adams NHS
   d. Vanderbilt Mansion NHS
   e. McLoughlin House NHS
   f. Gloria Dei Church NHS
   g. Touro Synagogue NHS
   h. San Jose Mission NHS
   i. Golden Spike NHS
   j. Whitman Mission NHS

   (1) Kentucky
   (2) Massachusetts
   (3) New York
   (4) New York
   (5) Oregon
   (6) Pennsylvania
   (7) Rhode Island
   (8) Texas
   (9) Utah
   (10) Washington

87. In what states are the following beaches?

   a. Coney Island
   b. Padre Island
   c. Bar Harbor
   d. Calumet Park
   e. Biloxi
   f. Pismo Beach
   g. Daytona Beach
   h. Waikiki Beach
   i. Asbury Park
   j. Sea Island

   (1) California
   (2) Florida
   (3) Georgia
   (4) Hawaii
   (5) Illinois
   (6) Maine
   (7) Mississippi
   (8) New Jersey
   (9) New York
   (10) Texas

88. In what states are the following areas, parks, centers and suburbs?

   a. Peachtree Center
   b. Shaker Heights
   c. Golden Triangle
   d. French Quarter
   e. Nob Hill
   f. The "Loop"
   g. Brookline
   h. Constitution Plaza)

   (1) California (San Francisco)
   (2) Connecticut (Hartford)
   (3) Georgia (Atlanta)
   (4) Illinois (Chicago)
   (5) Louisiana (New Orleans)
   (6) Massachusetts (Boston)
   (7) Ohio (Cleveland)
   (8) Pennsylvania (Pittsburgh)

89. In what states are the following universities located?

a. Baylor
b. Bradley
c. Brown
d. De Paul
e. Duquesne
f. Furman
g. Gonzaga
h. Kent State
i. Marquette
j. Purdue
k. Rice
l. Stanford

(1) California (Palo Alto)
(2) Illinois (Peoria)
(3) Illinois (Chicago)
(4) Indiana (Lafayette)
(5) Ohio
(6) Pennsylvania (Pittsburgh)
(7) Rhode Island (Providence)
(8) South Carolina (Greenville)
(9) Texas (Houston)
(10) Texas (Waco)
(11) Washington (Spokane)
(12) Wisconsin (Milwaukee)

90. In what states are the following?

a. Teapot Dome
b. Niagara Falls
c. Painted Desert
d. Craters of the Moon
e. Biltmore Mansion
f. Pentagon
g. Hells Half Acre
h. Astrodome

(1) Arizona
(2) Idaho
(3) New York
(4) North Carolina
(5) Texas
(6) Virginia
(7) Wyoming
(8) Wyoming

91. In what states are the following first seven established American universities?

a. Harvard (1636)
b. William and Mary (1693)
c. Yale (1701)
d. Pennsylvania (1740)
e. Princeton (1746)
f. Washington and Lee (1749)
g. Columbia (1754)

(1) Connecticut
(2) Massachusetts
(3) New Jersey
(4) New York
(5) Pennsylvania
(6) Virginia
(7) Virginia

92. In what states are the following tourist railroads?

Part I:
   a. Roaring Camp & Big Trees Narrow-Gauge Railroad
   b. Cumbres & Toltec Scenic Railroad
   c. Sumpter Valley Railroad
   d. Oil Creek & Titusville Railroad
   e. Lamoille Valley Railroad
   f. Black Hills Central Railroad
   g. Mt. Washington Cog Railroad

   (1) California
   (2) Colorado and New Mexico
   (3) New Hampshire
   (4) Oregon
   (5) Pennsylvania
   (6) South Dakota
   (7) Vermont

Part II:
   a. Fremont & Elkhorn Valley Railroad
   b. Big South Fork Scenic Railway
   c. Boone & Scenic Valley Railroad
   d. Little River Railroad
   e. Hart County Scenic Railway
   f. Cripple Creek & Victor Narrow Gauge Railroad
   g. Yreka Western Railroad (Blue Goose)

   (1) California
   (2) Colorado
   (3) Georgia
   (4) Indiana
   (5) Iowa
   (6) Kentucky
   (7) Nebraska

93. Match the following state historic parks to the state.

Part I:
   a. Camp Floyd and Stagecoach Inn State Park
   b. Mills Mansion State Historic Site
   c. Joss House State Historic Park
   d. Mormon State Historic Monument
   e. Fort Fetterman State Historic Site

   (1) California (Weaverville)
   (2) Nevada (Genoa)
   (3) New York (Hyde Park)
   (4) Utah (Fairfield)
   (5) Wyoming (Douglas)

Part II:
   a. Bulow Plantation Ruins and State Historic Site
   b. Tannehill Historic State Park
   c. Goliad State Historical Park
   d. Jarrell Plantation State Historic Site
   e. Bennett Place State Historic Site

   (1) Alabama (McCalla)
   (2) Florida (Bunnell)
   (3) Georgia (Juliette)
   (4) North Carolina (Durham)
   (5) Texas

Part III:
  a. Colonial Pemaquid State Historic Site
  b. Ash Hollow State Historic Park
  c. Jerome State Historic Park
  d. Steuben House State Historic Site
  e. Black Hawk State Historic Site

(1) Arizona
(2) Illinois (Rock Island)
(3) Maine
(4) Nebraska (Lewellen)
(5) New Jersey (Hackensack)

Part IV:
  a. Corydon State Historic Site
  b. Boone's Lick State Historic Site
  c. Pawnee Rock State Historic Site
  d. Old Mulkey Meetinghouse State Historic Site
  e. Alex Haley State Historic Site and Museum

(1) Indiana
(2) Kansas
(3) Kentucky (Tompkinsville)
(4) Missouri
(5) Tennessee (Hendersonville)

94. The following graves and tombs are located in which states?

Part I:
  a. Henry Clay
  b. Carl Sandburg
  c. Walt Whitman
  d. Molly Pitcher
  e. Paul Revere
  f. Kit Carson

(1) Illinois (Galesburg)
(2) Kentucky (Lexington)
(3) Massachusetts (Boston)
(4) New Jersey (Camden)
(5) New Mexico (Taos)
(6) Pennsylvania (Carlisle)

Part II:
  a. Ethan Allen
  b. Patrick Henry
  c. Edgar Allan Poe
  d. Judge Roy Bean
  e. Mark Twain
  f. Meriwether Lewis

(1) Maryland (Baltimore)
(2) New York (Elmira)
(3) Tennessee (Natchez Trace Parkway)
(4) Texas (Del Rio)
(5) Vermont (Burlington)
(6) Virginia (Brookneal)

95. In what states are the following carillons?

Part I:
- a. Hoover Tower
- b. Centennial Carillon Tower
- c. Bok Tower Gardens
- d. Leonidas Polk Carillon
- e. Mahanay Memorial Carillon Tower
- f. Brownell Memorial Park & Carillon

(1) California (Stanford University)
(2) Florida (Lake Wales)
(3) Iowa (Jefferson)
(4) Louisiana (Morgan City)
(5) Tennessee (Sewanee)
(6) Utah (Provo)

Part II:
- a. Davis Memorial Carillon
- b. Callie Self Memorial Carillon
- c. Washington Memorial National Carillon
- d. Burton Memorial Tower
- e. Thomas Rees Memorial Carillon
- f. Carroll Chimes Bell Tower

(1) Illinois (Springfield)
(2) Michigan (Ann Arbor)
(3) New York (Alfred)
(4) Ohio (Cincinnati)
(5) Pennsylvania (Valley Forge)
(6) South Carolina (Greenwood)

96. In what states are the following Indian mounds and remains?

Part I:
- a. Spiro Mounds Archeological State Park
- b. Toltec Mounds State Park
- c. Effigy Mounds National Monument
- d. Grave Creek Mound
- e. Caddoan Mounds State Historic Site
- f. Serpent Mound

(1) Arkansas (Scott)
(2) Iowa
(3) Ohio (Locust Grove)
(4) Oklahoma
(5) Texas (Alto)
(6) West Virginia (Moundsville)

Part II:
- a. Angel Mounds State Historic Site
- b. Etowah Indian Mounds State Historic Site
- c. Wickliffe Mounds
- d. Pinson Mounds State Archaeological Area
- e. Lizard Mound County Park
- f. Tuzigoot National Monument

(1) Arizona
(2) Georgia (Cartersville)
(3) Indiana (Evansville)
(4) Kentucky
(5) Tennessee
(6) Wisconsin (West Bend)

97. In what states are the following observatories and planetariums?

Part I:
   a. Griffith Observatory and Planetarium
   b. Fleischmann Planetarium
   c. Kitt Peak National Observatory
   d. The Adler Planetarium
   e. William M. Staerkel Planetarium
   f. Burke Baker Planetarium

(1) Arizona
(2) California (Los Angeles)
(3) Illinois (Champaign-Urbana)
(4) Illinois (Chicago)
(5) Nevada (Reno)
(6) Texas (Houston)

Part II:
   a. Hopkins Planetarium
   b. Fels Planetarium
   c. Libby Flats Observatory
   d. The Fiske Planetarium
   e. Washburn Observatory
   f. Hayden Planetarium

(1) Colorado (Boulder)
(2) New York (New York City)
(3) Pennsylvania (Philadelphia)
(4) Virginia (Roanoke)
(5) Wisconsin (Madison)
(6) Wyoming (Laramie)

98. In what states are the following mines?

Part I:
   a. Kennecott's Bingham Canyon Mine
   b. Mollie Kathleen Gold Mine
   c. Iron Mountain Iron Mine
   d. Gore Mountain Garnet Mine
   e. Empire Mine State Historic Park

(1) California (Grass Valley)
(2) Colorado (Cripple Creek)
(3) Michigan
(4) New York (North Creek)
(5) Utah

Part II:
   a. Vinegar Hill Lead Mine
   b. Queen Mine
   c. The Homestake Gold Mine
   d. Hull-Rust Mine
   e. Sterling Hill Mine

(1) Arizona (Bisbee)
(2) Illinois (Galena)
(3) Minnesota (Hibbing)
(4) New Jersey (Ogdensburg)
(5) South Dakota

99. In what states are the following marine locks?

Part I:
   a. Plaquemine Lock
   b. Columbus Lock
   c. Great Bridge Locks
   d. Starved Rock Lock
   e. Sandy Lake Lock

(1) Illinois (Utica)
(2) Louisiana
(3) Minnesota (McGregor)
(4) Mississippi
(5) Virginia (Chesapeake)

Part II:

a. Murray Lock   (1) Arkansas (Little Rock)

b. Soo Locks   (2) Michigan (Sault Ste. Marie)

c. John Day Lock   (3) New York (Massena)

d. Lower Monumental Lock   (4) Oregon (Rufus)

e. Bertrand Snell Lock   (5) Washington (Kahlotus)

100. In what states are the following National Recreation Areas?

Part I:

a. Cuyahoga Valley NRA   (1) Arizona

b. Sawtooth NRA   (2) Georgia

c. Glen Canyon NRA   (3) Idaho

d. Chattahoochee River NRA   (4) New Jersey

e. Delaware Water Gap NRA   (5) Ohio

Part II:

a. Chickasaw NRA   (1) California

b. Whiskeytown-Shasta-Trinity NRA   (2) Colorado

c. Lake Chelan NRA   (3) Oklahoma

d. Arapaho NRA   (4) Virginia

e. Mount Rogers NRA   (5) Washington

101. In what states are the following Indian reservations?

Part I:

a. Pyramid Lake   (1) Colorado

b. Quinault   (2) Kansas

c. Ouray   (3) Michigan

d. Laguna   (4) Minnesota

e. Rocky Boy's   (5) Montana

f. Fort Totten   (6) Nevada

g. Potawatami   (7) New Mexico

h. Southern Ute   (8) North Dakota

i. Keweenaw Bay   (9) Utah

j. White Earth   (10) Washington

Part II:

a. Hoopa Valley	(1) Arizona
b. Warm Springs	(2) California
c. Fort Hall	(3) Florida
d. Papago	(4) Idaho
e. Wind River	(5) Nebraska
f. Winnebago	(6) Oklahoma
g. Pine Ridge	(7) Oregon
h. Osage	(8) South Dakota
i. Brighton	(9) Wisconsin
j. Oneida	(10) Wyoming

102. In what states are the following man-made reservoirs?

a. Lake Oahe	(1) California
b. Lake Koocanusa	(2) Kentucky
c. Lake Shasta	(3) Louisiana
d. Lake Sakakawea	(4) Montana
e. Toledo Bend Lake	(5) North Dakota
f. Cumberland Lake	(6) South Dakota

103. In what states are the following embankment dams?

a. Fort Peck	(1) California
b. Garrison	(2) Montana
c. Fort Randall	(3) Nebraska
d. Castaic	(4) New Mexico
e. Cochiti	(5) North Dakota
f. Kingsley	(6) South Dakota

104. In what states are the following dams?

a. Detroit	(1) California
b. Hungry Horse	(2) Colorado
c. Morrow Point	(3) Georgia
d. Shasta	(4) Idaho
e. Mossyrock	(5) Montana
f. Anderson Ranch	(6) New York
g. Carters	(7) Oregon
h. Jocassee	(8) South Carolina
i. Merriman	(9) Utah
j. Flaming Gorge	(10) Washington

105. In what states are the following underwater vehicular tunnels?
    a. Callahan Tunnel (5,046 feet)
    b. Holland Tunnel (8,557 feet)
    c. Thimble Shoal Channel (8,187 feet)
    d. Fort McHenry Tunnel (7,200 feet)

106. In what states are the following land vehicular tunnels?
    a. Caldecott (3,371 feet)
    b. Tuscaror (5,400 feet)
    c. East River Mountain (5,412 feet)
    d. Dingess Tunnel (3,400 feet)

107. In what states are or were the following lighthouses?

Part I:			
	a. Hecata Head	(1)	Alaska
	b. Fire Island	(2)	California
	c. Point Arena	(3)	Maine
	d. Cape May	(4)	Mississippi
	e. Cape Hatteras	(5)	New Jersey
	f. Cape Elizabeth	(6)	New York
	g. Cape St. Elias	(7)	North Carolina
	h. Biloxi	(8)	Oregon

Part II:			
	a. Rock of Ages	(1)	Florida
	b. Jupiter	(2)	Georgia
	c. Tybee	(3)	Massachusetts
	d. Minot's Ledge	(4)	Michigan
	e. Whaleback	(5)	New Hampshire
	f. Castle Hill	(6)	Rhode Island
	g. Haig Point	(7)	South Carolina
	h. Cape Hebry	(8)	Virginia

Part III:			
	a. Bolivar Point	(1)	California
	b. Split Rock	(2)	Connecticut
	c. Stannard Rock	(3)	Maine
	d. New London	(4)	Massachusetts
	e. Grays Harbor	(5)	Minnesota
	f. Pigeon Point	(6)	Michigan
	g. Boone Island	(7)	Texas
	h. Annisquam	(8)	Washington

108. In what future states were the following American Revolutionary War battlefields?

a. Ticonderoga	(1) Connecticut
b. Yorktown	(2) Delaware
c. Germantown	(3) New Jersey
d. Cowpens	(4) New York
e. Monmouth	(5) North Carolina
f. Danbury	(6) Pennsylvania
g. Cooch's Bridge	(7) South Carolina
h. Moore's Creek Bridge	(8) Virginia

109. In what states were the following forts established?

Part I:

a. For Ord	(1) California
b. Fort Leavenworth	(2) Georgia
c. Fort Laramie	(3) Kansas
d. Fort Bliss	(4) New York
e. Fort Benning	(5) Texas
f. Fort Ticonderoga	(6) Wyoming

Part II:

a. Fort Vincennes	(1) Indiana
b. Fort Mifflin	(2) Nevada
c. Fort Simcoe	(3) Oregon
d. Fort Meade	(4) Pennsylvania
e. Fort Champoeg	(5) South Dakota
f. Fort Churchill	(6) Washington

110. In what states were the following military installations and command centers established?

a. Great Lakes Naval Training Station	(1) Alabama
b. Jefferson Proving Ground	(2) Florida
c. Cape Kennedy Rocket Station	(3) Illinois
d. Aberdeen Proving Ground	(4) Maryland
e. White Sands Missile Range	(5) Mississippi
f. Anniston Army Depot	(6) New Mexico

111. In what states are or were the following Air Force bases?

Part I:	a. Lake Charles Air Force Base	(1) California
	b. Langley Air Force Base	(2) Hawaii
	c. McConnell Air Force Base	(3) Kansas
	d. Hickam Air Force Base	(4) Louisiana
	e. Hill Air Force Base	(5) Nebraska
	f. Offut Air Force Base	(6) Utah
	g. Edwards Air Force Base	(7) Virginia

Part II:	a. Elmendorf Air Force Base	(1) Alaska
	b. Lowry Air Force Base	(2) Colorado
	c. Nellis Air Force Base	(3) Nevada
	d. Ellsworth Air Force Base	(4) New Mexico
	e. Holloman Air Force Base	(5) New York
	f. Griffiss Air Force Base	(6) Ohio
	g. Wright-Patterson Air Force Base	(7) South Dakota

112. In what states are the following missions?

a. Mission of Nombre de Dios	(1) Arizona (Tucson)
b. Lahaina Jodo Mission	(2) California (King City)
c. Shawnee Methodist Mission	(3) Florida (St. Augustine)
d. Mission San Xavier del Bac	(4) Hawaii
e. Mission of San Agustin de Isleta	(5) Kansas (Fairway)
f. Mission San Antonio de Padua	(6) New Mexico (Albuquerque)
g. Mission San Francisco de la Espada	(7) Texas (San Antonio)

113. In which states are the following National Parks?

Part I:	a. Mammoth Cave	(1) Alaska
	b. Capitol Reef	(2) Florida
	c. North Cascades	(3) Hawaii
	d. Glacier	(4) Kentucky
	e. Badlands	(5) Montana
	f. Theodore Roosevelt	(6) North Dakota
	g. Biscayne	(7) Oregon
	h. Crater Lake	(8) South Dakota
	i. Haleakala	(9) Utah
	j. Denali	(10) Washington

Part II:
    a. Big Bend
    b. Arches
    c. Everglades
    d. Lassen Volcanic
    e. Mount Rainier
    f. Petrified Forest
    g. Rocky Mountain
    h. Voyageurs
    i. Hot Springs
    j. Carlsbad Caverns

(1) Arizona
(2) Arkansas
(3) California
(4) Colorado
(5) Florida
(6) Minnesota
(7) New Mexico
(8) Texas
(9) Utah
(10) Washington

Part III:
    a. Kings Canyon
    b. Shenandoah
    c. Canyonlands
    d. Grand Teton
    e. Isle Royale
    f. Acadia
    g. Mesa Verde
    h. Guadalupe Mountains
    i. Wind Cave
    j. Olympic

(1) California
(2) Colorado
(3) Maine
(4) Michigan
(5) South Dakota
(6) Texas
(7) Utah
(8) Virginia
(9) Washington
(10) Wyoming

114. The following signers of the Declaration of Independence represented which future states (the names of these future states do not appear in the original document)?

Part I:
    a. Samuel Adams
    b. Francis Hopkinson
    c. Richard Henry Lee
    d. Benjamin Rush
    e. Edward Rutledge
    f. Roger Sherman
    g. Samuel Chase

(1) Connecticut
(2) Maryland
(3) Massachusetts
(4) New Jersey
(5) Pennsylvania
(6) South Carolina
(7) Virginia

Part II:
    a. Stephen Hopkins
    b. Lyman Hall
    c. William Hooper
    d. George Read
    e. Josiah Bartlett
    f. Lewis Morris

(1) Delaware
(2) Georgia
(3) New Hampshire
(4) New York
(5) North Carolina
(6) Rhode Island

115. The following signers of the Federal Constitution represented which future states?

Part I:			
	a. Alexander Hamilton	(1)	Connecticut
	b. Robert Morris	(2)	Massachusetts
	c. Rufus King	(3)	New Hampshire
	d. William S. Johnson	(4)	New York
	e. Nicholas Gilman	(5)	Pennsylvania
	f. John Blair	(6)	Virginia

Part II:			
	a. Abraham Baldwin	(1)	Delaware
	b. John Dickinson	(2)	Georgia
	c. William Blount	(3)	Maryland
	d. Charles Pinckney	(4)	New Jersey
	e. William Livingston	(5)	North Carolina
	f. James McHenry	(6)	South Carolina

116. In what states are the following?

Part I:			
	a. Kings Ranch	(1)	Colorado
	b. Fontana Dam	(2)	Missouri
	c. Hannibal (Mark Twain's home)	(3)	Nebraska
	d. Boys Town	(4)	New Mexico
	e. Ruth	(5)	Nevada
	f. Betsy Ross House	(6)	North Carolina
	g. Block Island (resort island)	(7)	Oregon
	h. Acoma Pueblo	(8)	Pennsylvania
	i. Tillamook (cheese factories)	(9)	Rhode Island
	j. Cripple Creek (mining town)	(10)	Texas

Part II:			
	a. Bristol Bay	(1)	Alaska
	b. Independence Rock	(2)	Arizona
	c. Big Rock Candy Mountain	(3)	Florida
	d. Coral Gables	(4)	Maryland
	e. Haggerstown	(5)	Michigan
	f. The Alamo	(6)	Pennsylvania
	g. The Hermitage	(7)	Tennessee
	h. Valley Forge	(8)	Texas
	i. Greenfield Village	(9)	Utah
	j. Oak Creek Canyon	(10)	Wyoming

Part III:

a. International Peace Garden
b. Ausable Chasm
c. Puget Sound
d. Audubon State Park
e. Cahokia Mounds State Park
f. Garrison Dam
g. Berkeley Springs
h. Natchez
i. Donner Pass
j. Plymouth Rock

(1) California
(2) Illinois
(3) Kentucky
(4) Massachusetts
(5) Mississippi
(6) New York
(7) North Dakota
(8) North Dakota
(9) Washington
(10) West Virginia

117. Name the state in which the following authors were born.

Part I:

a. Sinclair Lewis
b. Jack London
c. Henry Wadsworth Longfellow
d. Herman Melville
e. Margaret Mitchell
f. Dorothy Parker

(1) California (San Francisco)
(2) Georgia (Atlanta)
(3) Maine (Portland)
(4) Minnesota (Sauk Centre)
(5) New Jersey (West End)
(6) New York (New York City)

Part II:

a. Edgar Allan Poe
b. James Whitcomb Riley
c. Carl Sandburg
d. Damon Runyon
e. Thomas Stearns Eliot
f. Upton Sinclair

(1) Illinois (Galesburg)
(2) Indiana (Greenfield)
(3) Kansas (Manhattan)
(4) Maryland (Baltimore)
(5) Massachusetts (Boston)
(6) Missouri (St. Louis)

Part III:

a. Louisa May Alcott
b. Sherwood Anderson
c. Ernest Hemingway
d. Samual Longhorne Clemens
e. William Cuthbert Faulkner
f. Edna Ferber

(1) Illinois (Oak Park)
(2) Michigan (Kalamazoo)
(3) Mississippi (New Albany)
(4) Missouri (Florida)
(5) Ohio (Camden)
(6) Pennsylvania (Germantown)

Part IV:

a. F. Scott Fitzgerald	(1) California (Salinas)
b. Bret Harte	(2) Connecticut (Litchfield)
c. Nathaniel Hawthorne	(3) Massachusetts (Salem)
d. John Steinbeck	(4) Minnesota (St. Paul)
e. Harriet Beecher Stowe	(5) New York (Albany)
f. Thornton Wilder	(6) Wisconsin (Madison)

118. Name the states or future states in which the following famous people were born.

Part I:

a. Lew(is) Wallace	(1) Connecticut (Coventry)
b. Carry Amelia Nation	(2) Georgia (Savannah)
c. Nathan Hale	(3) Indiana (Brookville)
d. Frederick Douglass	(4) Kansas (Atchison)
e. Amelia Mary Earhart	(5) Kentucky (Gerrard County)
f. John C. Fremont	(6) Maryland (Tuckahoe)

Part II:

a. Tennessee Williams	(1) Massachusetts (Oxford)
b. William Techumseh Sherman	(2) Mississippi (Columbus)
	(3) Missouri (Maryville)
c. Dolley Payne Madison	(4) New Hampshire (Salisbury)
d. Dale Carnegie	(5) North Carolina (Guilford City)
e. Clara Barton	
f. Daniel Webster	(6) Ohio (Lancaster)

Part III:

a. John Marshall	(1) Pennsylvania (Lawrenceville)
b. Brigham Young	(2) Rhode Island (South Kingston)
c. Oliver Hazard Perry	(3) Tennessee (Pall Mall)
d. Stephen Collins Foster	(4) Vermont (Whitingham)
e. Frank Lloyd Wright	(5) Virginia (Fauquier City)
f. Alvin York	(6) Wisconsin (Richland Center)

119. Match the festival to the state in which it takes place.

Part I:

a. C&O Canal Boat Festival	(1) California (Sonoma County)
b. Daffodil Festival	(2) Georgia (Toombs County)
c. Vidalia Onion Festival	(3) Maryland (Allegany County)
d. Nordicfest	(4) Massachusetts (Barnstable County)
e. Musikfest	
f. Valley of the Moon Vintage Festival	(5) Montana (Lincoln County)
	(6) Pennsylvania (Northampton County)

Part II:

a. Woolly Worm Festival
b. Rayne Frog Festival
c. National Hobo Convention
d. Bratwurst Festival
e. Speckled Perch Festival
f. Rutabaga Festival

(1) Florida (Okeechobee County)
(2) Iowa (Hancock County)
(3) Louisiana (Acadia Parish)
(4) North Carolina (Avery County)
(5) Ohio (Crawford County)
(6) Wisconsin (Barron County)

Part III:

a. The Whole Enchilada Fiesta
b. Narcissus Festival
c. National Asparagus Festival
d. International Celtic Festival
e. Festival Italiano
f. World's Biggest Fish Fry

(1) Connecticut (New London County)
(2) Hawaii (Honolulu)
(3) Michigan (Oceana County)
(4) New Mexico (Dona Ana County)
(5) New York (Greene County)
(6) Tennessee (Henry County)

120. The National Statuary Hall in the United States Capitol building presently consists of 95 statues contributed by fifty states. Forty-five states have contributed two statues each. Five states are eligible to donate one additional statue each. Which five states are they?

121. The proposal to create a National Statuary Hall became law on July 2, 1864. The following names are to be matched with the states they represent. Each state is represented at least once.

Part I:

a. Jonathan Trumbull
b. Eusebio Francisco Kino
c. Stephen Austin
d. Julius Sterling Morton
e. John Stark
f. Will Rogers
g. James Harlan
h. Father Damien
i. John Burke
j. Father Junipero Serra

(1) Arizona
(2) California
(3) Connecticut
(4) Hawaii
(5) Iowa
(6) Nebraska
(7) New Hampshire
(8) North Dakota
(9) Oklahoma
(10) Texas

Part II:

a. Charles Brantley Aycock

b. John Winthrop

c. Lewis Wallace

d. Jacques Marquette

e. Ernest Gruening

f. Francis Harrison Pierpont

g. John Middleton Clayton

h. Brigham Young

i. Edward Douglas White

j. Esther Hobart Morris

(1) Alaska

(2) Delaware

(3) Indiana

(4) Louisiana

(5) Massachusetts

(6) North Carolina

(7) Utah

(8) West Virginia

(9) Wisconsin

(10) Wyoming

Part III:

a. Jacob Collamer

b. John James Ingalls

c. Crawford W. Long

d. Patrick Anthony McCarran

e. Lewis Cass

f. William Allen

g. Philip Kearny

h. Joseph Ward

i. George Clinton

j. Maria L. Sanford

(1) Georgia

(2) Kansas

(3) Michigan

(4) Minnesota

(5) Nevada

(6) New Jersey

(7) New York

(8) Ohio

(9) South Dakota

(10) Vermont

Part IV:

a. Thomas Hart Benton

b. Dennis Chavez

c. Robert Fulton

d. Hannibal Hamlin

e. Robert E. Lee

f. Charles Carroll of Carrolton

g. John Sevier

h. Frances E. Willard

i. Uriah Milton Rose

j. Edmund Kirby Smith

(1) Arkansas

(2) Florida

(3) Illinois

(4) Maine

(5) Maryland

(6) Missouri

(7) New Mexico

(8) Pennsylvania

(9) Tennessee

(10) Virginia

Part V:

a. Marcus Whitman	(1) Alabama
b. William Edgar Borah	(2) Colorado
c. Jason Lee	(3) Idaho
d. Nathaniel Greene	(4) Kentucky
e. Jefferson Davis	(5) Mississippi
f. John Caldwell Calhous	(6) Montana
g. Charles Marion Russell	(7) Oregon
h. Henry Clay	(8) Rhode Island
i. Florence Sabin	(9) South Carolina
j. Joseph Wheeler	(10) Washington

Part VI:

a. Ethan Allen	(1) Connecticut
b. Robert M. La Follette	(2) Hawaii
c. Roger Williams	(3) Louisiana
d. Huey Pierce Long	(4) Massachusetts
e. William Jennings Bryan	(5) Nebraska
f. King Kamehameha I	(6) New Hampshire
g. Sequoya	(7) Oklahoma
h. Samuel Adams	(8) Rhode Island
i. Daniel Webster	(9) Tennessee
j. Roger Sherman	(10) Texas
k. Sam Houston	(12) Vermont
l. Andrew Jackson	(13) Wisconsin

ANSWERS TO
PEOPLE, PARKS AND PLACES

1. Delaware

2. Alaska (Wrangell-St. Elias National Park and Preserve – 13.2 million acres)

3. California (Anza-Borrego – 600,000 acres)

4. Pennsylvania (Hershey)

5. Alaska (purchased from Russia in 1867 for $7,200,000)

6. South Dakota (Mitchell)

7. Arizona (Lake Havasu City)

8. California (San Marino)

9. Minnesota

10. Montana (Glacier National Park)

11. Arizona

12. New Jersey (Menlo Park and West Orange)

13. Louisiana

14. Idaho and Oregon

15. Florida and Georgia

16. Alaska

17. New York

18. Massachusetts

19. Idaho, Montana, Wyoming (Yellowstone National Park)

20. North Carolina

21. Mississippi (Biloxi)

22. a. New York (West Point)
    b. Maryland (Annapolis)
    c. Colorado (Colorado Springs)
    d. Connecticut (New London)
    e. New York (Kings Point)

23. New Hampshire (North Salem)

24. Tennessee (Nashville)

25. Washington

26. North Carolina (Concord)

27. Montana

28. New Jersey

29. Florida (with an increase of 27.9 percent)

30. Wyoming

31. Arizona, California, New Mexico, Oklahoma

32. New Hampshire (established the first system of birth registration with records on file for 1640, shortly after the colony was established)

33. New Jersey and New York (navigable waterfront of 755 miles)

34. Arizona (Fountain Hills – maximum height 625 feet)

35. Massachusetts

36. North Carolina

37. New York

38. Texas (Denison)

39. Virginia

40. Tennessee (Nashville)

41. Maryland

42. Virginia

43. Arizona (Navajo)

44. Ohio

45. Virginia

46. New Hampshire, Rhode Island, Vermont

47. New York

48. Ohio (Dayton)

49. Virginia

50. Connecticut (completed in 1841 - 178 feet – spans Housatonic River on Rt. 128 in West Cornwall)

51. Washington

52. Pennsylvania

53. Georgia

54. Missouri

55. Kentucky

56. Tennessee (Dayton)

57. New Jersey (Peninsula)

58. New York

59. Oklahoma

60. Florida (Everglades)

61. Montana

62. Arkansas

63. Colorado (Denver)

64. Arizona

65. Alaska

66. Alabama

67. Iowa (Sioux City)

68. California (Alcatraz)

69. Iowa (Hoover)

70. Utah (Promentary Point)

71. Vermont

72. Virginia

73. Ohio

74. Massachusetts and New York

75. Wyoming

76. California, Connecticut, Delaware, Iowa, Minnesota, Missouri, Montana, North Carolina, North Dakota, New Mexico, Oregon, Pennsylvania, West Virginia

77. Alaska, Arkansas, Louisiana, North Carolina, Oklahoma, Texas, Utah, Wyoming

78. a. Florida
    b. Texas
    c. California
    d. Alabama

79. a. (3) Nevada
    b. (1) California
    c. (2) Idaho
    d. (6) Wyoming
    e. (4) Oregon
    f. (5) Utah

80. a. (1) California
    b. (5) New York
    c. (6) Ohio
    d. (2) Indiana
    e. (7) Pennsylvania
    f. (3) Iowa
    g. (4) Michigan

81. a. (6) New York
    b. (1) California
    c. (3) Hawaii
    d. (2) Florida
    e. (7) New York
    f. (8) Pennsylvania
    g. (4) Illinois
    h. (5) Minnesota

82. a. (4) Iowa
    b. (3) Georgia
    c. (7) Missouri
    d. (5) Kansas
    e. (9) Texas
    f. (6) Massachusetts
    g. (1) California
    h. (2) California
    i. (8) New York

83. Part I: a. (2) Georgia
             b. (4) New York
             c. (1) California
             d. (5) Washington
             e. (3) Massachusetts

    Part II: a. (1) Connecticut
             b. (4) Ohio
             c. (5) Virginia
             d. (2) Minnesota
             e. (3) New York

84. Part I: a. (4) New Mexico
             b. (3) Missouri
             c. (2) Kentucky
             d. (6) Virginia
             e. (1) Georgia
             f. (5) Tennessee

    Part II: a. (3) Mississippi
             b. (6) West Virginia
             c. (2) Maryland
             d. (5) Pennsylvania
             e. (4) Oklahoma
             f. (1) Louisiana

85. a. (7) Pennsylvania
    b. (6) North Carolina
    c. (2) Arkansas
    d. (9) Tennessee
    e. (10) Virginia
    f. (5) Mississippi
    g. (4) Maryland
    h. (1) Alabama
    i. (8) South Carolina
    j. (3) Georgia

86. a. (3) New York
    b. (1) Kentucky
    c. (2) Massachusetts
    d. (4) New York
    e. (5) Oregon
    f. (6) Pennsylvania
    g. (7) Rhode Island
    h. (8) Texas
    i. (9) Utah
    j. (10) Washington

87. a. (9) New York
    b. (10) Texas
    c. (6) Maine
    d. (5) Illinois
    e. (7) Mississippi
    f. (1) California
    g. (2) Florida
    h. (4) Hawaii
    i. (8) New Jersey
    j. (3) Georgia

88. a. (3) Georgia
    b. (7) Ohio
    c. (8) Pennsylvania
    d. (5) Louisiana
    e. (1) California
    f. (4) Illinois
    g. (6) Massachusetts
    h. (2) Connecticut

89. a. (9) Texas
    b. (2) Illinois
    c. (7) Rhode Island
    d. (3) Illinois
    e. (6) Pennsylvania
    f. (8) South Carolina
    g. (11) Washington
    h. (5) Ohio
    i. (12) Wisconsin
    j. (4) Indiana
    k. (10) Texas
    l. (1) California

90. a. (7) Wyoming
    b. (3) New York
    c. (1) Arizona
    d. (2) Idaho
    e. (4) North Carolina
    f. (6) Virginia
    g. (8) Wyoming
    h. (5) Texas

91. a. (2) Massachusetts
    b. (6) Virginia
    c. (1) Connecticut
    d. (5) Pennsylvania
    e. (3) New Jersey
    f. (7) Virginia
    g. (4) New York

92. Part I:
a. (1) California
b. (2) Colorado & New Mexico
c. (4) Oregon
d. (5) Pennsylvania
e. (7) Vermont
f. (6) South Dakota
g. (3) New Hampshire

Part II:
a. (7) Nebraska
b. (6) Kentucky
c. (5) Iowa
d. (4) Indiana
e. (3) Georgia
f. (2) Colorado
g. (1) California

93. Part I:
a. (4) Utah
b. (3) New York
c. (1) California
d. (2) Nevada
e. (5) Wyoming

Part II:
a. (2) Florida
b. (1) Alabama
c. (5) Texas
d. (3) Georgia
e. (4) North Carolina

Part III:
a. (3) Maine
b. (4) Nebraska
c. (1) Arizona
d. (5) New Jersey
e. (2) Illinois

Part IV:
a. (1) Indiana
b. (4) Missouri
c. (2) Kansas
d. (3) Kentucky
e. (5) Tennessee

94. Part I:
a. (2) Kentucky
b. (1) Illinois
c. (4) New Jersey
d. (6) Pennsylvania
e. (3) Massachusetts
f. (5) New Mexico

Part II:
a. (5) Vermont
b. (6) Virginia
c. (1) Maryland
d. (4) Texas
e. (2) New York
f. (3) Tennessee

95. Part I:
a. (1) California
b. (6) Utah
c. (2) Florida
d. (5) Tennessee
e. (3) Iowa
f. (4) Louisiana

Part II:
a. (3) New York
b. (6) South Carolina
c. (5) Pennsylvania
d. (2) Michigan
e. (1) Illinois
f. (4) Ohio

96. Part I:
a. (4) Oklahoma
b. (1) Arkansas
c. (2) Iowa
d. (6) West Virginia
e. (5) Texas
f. (3) Ohio

Part II:
a. (3) Indiana
b. (2) Georgia
c. (4) Kentucky
d. (5) Tennessee
e. (6) Wisconsin
f. (1) Arizona

97. Part I:
a. (2) California
b. (5) Nevada
c. (1) Arizona
d. (3) Illinois
e. (4) Illinois
f. (6) Texas

Part II:
a. (4) Virginia
b. (3) Pennsylvania
c. (6) Wyoming
d. (1) Colorado
e. (5) Wisconsin
f. (2) New York

98. Part I:
    a. (5) Utah
    b. (2) Colorado
    c. (3) Michigan
    d. (4) New York
    e. (1) California

    Part II:
    a. (2) Illinois
    b. (1) Arizona
    c. (5) South Dakota
    d. (3) Minnesota
    e. (4) New Jersey

99. Part I:
    a. (2) Louisiana
    b. (4) Mississippi
    c. (5) Virginia
    d. (1) Illinois
    e. (3) Minnesota

    Part II:
    a. (1) Arkansas
    b. (2) Michigan
    c. (4) Oregon
    d. (5) Washington
    e. (3) New York

100. Part I:
    a. (5) Ohio
    b. (3) Idaho
    c. (1) Arizona
    d. (2) Georgia
    e. (4) New Jersey

    Part II:
    a. (3) Oklahoma
    b. (1) California
    c. (5) Washington
    d. (2) Colorado
    e. (4) Virginia

101. Part I:
    a. (6) Nevada
    b. (10) Washington
    c. (9) Utah
    d. (7) New Mexico
    e. (5) Montana
    f. (8) North Dakota
    g. (2) Kansas
    h. (1) Colorado
    i. (3) Michigan
    j. (4) Minnesota

Part II:
    a. (2) California
    b. (7) Oregon
    c. (4) Idaho
    d. (1) Arizona
    e. (10) Wyoming
    f. (5) Nebraska
    g. (8) South Dakota
    h. (6) Oklahoma
    i. (3) Florida
    j. (9) Wisconsin

102.
    a. (6) South Dakota
    b. (4) Montana
    c. (1) California
    d. (5) North Dakota
    e. (3) Louisiana
    f. (2) Kentucky

103.
    a. (2) Montana
    b. (5) North Dakota
    c. (6) South Dakota
    d. (1) California
    e. (4) New Mexico
    f. (3) Nebraska

104.
    a. (7) Oregon
    b. (5) Montana
    c. (2) Colorado
    d. (1) California
    e. (10) Washington
    f. (4) Idaho
    g. (3) Georgia
    h. (8) South Carolina
    i. (6) New York
    j. (9) Utah

105.
    a. Massachusetts
    b. New York
    c. Virginia
    d. Maryland

106.
    a. California
    b. Pennsylvania
    c. Virginia
    d. West Virginia

107. Part I:
    a. (9) Oregon
    b. (7) New York
    c. (2) California
    d. (5) New Jersey
    e. (8) North Carolina
    f. (3) Maine
    g. (1) Alaska
    h. (4) Mississippi

Part II:
    a. (4) Michigan
    b. (1) Florida
    c. (2) Georgia
    d. (3) Massachusetts
    e. (5) New Hampshire
    f. (6) Rhode Island
    g. (7) South Carolina
    h. (8) Virginia

Part III:
    a. (7) Texas
    b. (5) Minnesota
    c. (6) Michigan
    d. (2) Connecticut
    e. (8) Washington
    f. (1) California
    g. (3) Maine
    h. (4) Massachusetts

108.
    a. (4) New York
    b. (8) Virginia
    c. (6) Pennsylvania
    d. (7) South Carolina
    e. (3) New Jersey
    f. (1) Connecticut
    g. (2) Delaware
    h. (5) North Carolina

109. Part I:
    a. (1) California
    b. (3) Kansas
    c. (6) Wyoming
    d. (5) Texas
    e. (2) Georgia
    f. (4) New York

Part II:
    a. (1) Indiana
    b. (4) Pennsylvania
    c. (6) Washington
    d. (5) South Dakota
    e. (3) Oregon
    f. (2) Nevada

110.
    a. (3) Illinois
    b. (5) Mississippi
    c. (2) Florida
    d. (4) Maryland
    e. (6) New Mexico
    f. (1) Alabama

111. Part I:
    a. (4) Louisiana
    b. (7) Virginia
    c. (3) Kansas
    d. (2) Hawaii
    e. (6) Utah
    f. (5) Nebraska
    g. (1) California

Part II:
    a. (1) Alaska
    b. (2) Colorado
    c. (3) Nevada
    d. (7) South Dakota
    e. (4) New Mexico
    f. (5) New York
    g. (6) Ohio

112.
    a. (3) Florida
    b. (4) Hawaii
    c. (5) Kansas
    d. (1) Arizona
    e. (6) New Mexico
    f. (2) California
    g. (7) Texas

113. Part I:
    a. (4) Kentucky
    b. (9) Utah
    c. (10) Washington
    d. (5) Montana
    e. (8) South Dakota
    f. (6) North Dakota
    g. (2) Florida
    h. (7) Oregon
    i. (3) Hawaii
    j. (1) Alaska

Part II: a. (8) Texas
b. (9) Utah
c. (5) Florida
d. (3) California
e. (10) Washington
f. (1) Arizona
g. (4) Colorado
h. (6) Minnesota
i. (2) Arkansas
j. (7) New Mexico

Part III: a. (1) California
b. (8) Virginia
c. (7) Utah
d. (10) Wyoming
e. (4) Michigan
f. (3) Maine
g. (2) Colorado
h. (6) Texas
i. (5) South Dakota
j. (9) Washington

114. Part I: a. (3) Massachusetts
b. (4) New Jersey
c. (7) Virginia
d. (5) Pennsylvania
e. (6) South Carolina
f. (1) Connecticut
g. (2) Maryland

Part II: a. (6) Rhode Island
b. (2) Georgia
c. (5) North Carolina
d. (1) Delaware
e. (3) New Hampshire
f. (4) New York

115. Part I: a. (4) New York
b. (5) Pennsylvania
c. (2) Massachusetts
d. (1) Connecticut
e. (3) New Hampshire
f. (6) Virginia

Part II: a. (2) Georgia
b. (1) Delaware
c. (5) North Carolina
d. (6) South Carolina
e. (4) New Jersey
f. (3) Maryland

116. Part I: a. (10) Texas
b. (6) North Carolina
c. (2) Missouri
d. (3) Nebraska
e. (5) Nevada
f. (8) Pennsylvania
g. (9) Rhode Island
h. (4) New Mexico
i. (7) Oregon
j. (1) Colorado

Part II: a. (1) Alaska
b. (10) Wyoming
c. (9) Utah
d. (3) Florida
e. (4) Maryland
f. (8) Texas
g. (7) Tennessee
h. (6) Pennsylvania
i. (5) Michigan
j. (2) Arizona

Part III: a. (7) North Dakota
b. (6) New York
c. (9) Washington
d. (3) Kentucky
e. (2) Illinois
f. (8) North Dakota
g. (10) West Virginia
h. (5) Mississippi
i. (1) California
j. (4) Massachusetts

117. Part I: a. (4) Minnesota
b. (1) California
c. (3) Maine
d. (6) New York
e. (2) Georgia
f. (5) New Jersey

Part II: a. (5) Massachusetts
b. (2) Indiana
c. (1) Illinois
d. (3) Kansas
e. (6) Missouri
f. (4) Maryland

Part III:
a. (6) Pennsylvania
b. (5) Ohio
c. (1) Illinois
d. (4) Missouri
e. (3) Mississippi
f. (2) Michigan

Part IV:
a. (4) Minnesota
b. (5) New York
c. (3) Massachusetts
d. (1) California
e. (2) Connecticut
f. (6) Wisconsin

118. Part I:
a. (3) Indiana
b. (5) Kentucky
c. (1) Connecticut
d. (6) Maryland
e. (4) Kansas
f. (2) Georgia

Part II:
a. (2) Mississippi
b. (6) Ohio
c. (5) North Carolina
d. (3) Missouri
e. (1) Massachusetts
f. (4) New Hampshire

Part III:
a. (5) Virginia
b. (4) Vermont
c. (2) Rhode Island
d. (1) Pennsylvania
e. (6) Wisconsin
f. (3) Tennessee

119. Part I:
a. (3) Maryland
b. (4) Massachusetts
c. (2) Georgia
d. (5) Montana
e. (6) Pennsylvania
f. (1) California

Part II:
a. (4) North Carolina
b. (3) Louisiana
c. (2) Iowa
d. (5) Ohio
e. (1) Florida
f. (6) Wisconsin

Part III:
a. (4) New Mexico
b. (2) Hawaii
c. (3) Michigan
d. (5) New York
e. (1) Connecticut
f. (6) Tennessee

120. Colorado, Nevada, New Mexico, North Dakota and Wyoming

121. Part I:
a. (3) Connecticut
b. (1) Arizona
c. (10) Texas
d. (6) Nebraska
e. (7) New Hampshire
f. (9) Oklahoma
g. (5) Iowa
h. (4) Hawaii
i. (8) North Dakota
j. (2) California

Part II:
a. (6) North Carolina
b. (5) Massachusetts
c. (3) Indiana
d. (9) Wisconsin
e. (1) Alaska
f. (8) West Virginia
g. (2) Delaware
h. (7) Utah
i. (4) Louisiana
j. (10) Wyoming

Part III:
a. (10) Vermont
b. (2) Kansas
c. (1) Georgia
d. (5) Nevada
e. (3) Michigan
f. (8) Ohio
g. (6) New Jersey
h. (9) South Dakota
i. (7) New York
j. (4) Minnesota

Part IV: a. (6) Missouri
           b. (7) New Mexico
           c. (8) Pennsylvania
           d. (4) Maine
           e. (10) Virginia
           f. (5) Maryland
           g. (9) Tennessee
           h. (3) Illinois
           i. (1) Arkansas
           j. (2) Florida

Part V: a. (10) Washington
           b. (3) Idaho
           c. (7) Oregon
           d. (8) Rhode Island
           e. (5) Mississippi
           f. (9) South Carolina
           g. (6) Montana
           h. (4) Kentucky
           i. (2) Colorado
           j. (1) Alabama

Part VI: a. (12) Vermont
           b. (13) Wisconsin
           c. (8) Rhode Island
           d. (3) Louisiana
           e. (5) Nebraska
           f. (2) Hawaii
           g. (7) Oklahoma
           h. (4) Massachusetts
           i. (6) New Hampshire
           j. (1) Connecticut
           k. (10) Texas
           l. (9) Tennessee

SIZES AND SHAPES

1. What state is shaped like a meat cleaver?

2. What state is made up of two large peninsulas?

3. What is the second smallest state?

4. What state has six straight sides?

5. Name six states that have well-known panhandles.

6. What is the largest inland state?

7. In what state is the largest country by area in the United States?

8. Not counting Alaska, which state is the longest and which is the widest?

9. What is the largest state east of the Mississippi River (land only)?

10. Name the third largest state.

11. What state is the smallest of the conterminous states west of Iowa?

12. Name the two states that are shaped like rectangles.

13. Name the state with the narrowest width (about a mile wide).

14. Counting fresh water and land, what is the largest state by area east of the Mississippi River?

15. In what state is the world's largest hanger?

16. The longest suspension bridge in the United States is in what state?

17. The longest highway in the interstate system is I-90. Which states are its termini?

18. In what state is the longest boat canal in the United States?

19. In what state is the largest earthfill dam in the United States?

20. The largest bell in the United States is found in what state?

21. In what state is the highest dam in the United States?

22. In what state is the longest main-line railroad tunnel in the United States?

23. The longest railroad bridge in the United States is in what state?

24. In what state is the world's longest stone arch bridge?

25. The longest road tunnel in the United States links what two states?

26. Where is the highest suspension bridge in the United States?

27. The following animal statues claim to be the world's largest. Match the states they are in.

   a. Road Runner
   b. Buffalo (Bison)
   c. Prairie Chicken
   d. Bug
   e. Shrimp
   f. Cow
   g. Bull
   h. Goose

   (1) Colorado (Colorado Springs)
   (2) Iowa (Audubon)
   (3) Minnesota (Rothsay)
   (4) Missouri (Sumner)
   (5) North Dakota (New Salem)
   (6) North Dakota (Jamestown)
   (7) Texas (Ft. Stockton)
   (8) Texas (Houston)

28. The following counties are the largest by size in their state. Match them to the states listed.

   Part I:
   a. Coconino
   b. McLean
   c. Fall River
   d. Harney
   e. McKenzie
   f. Osage
   g. St. Lawrence
   h. Aroostook

   (1) Arizona
   (2) Illinois
   (3) Maine
   (4) New York
   (5) North Dakota
   (6) Oklahoma
   (7) Oregon
   (8) South Dakota

   Part II:
   a. St. Louis
   b. Las Animas
   c. Union
   d. Worcester
   e. Nye
   f. Beaverhead
   g. Burlington
   h. Brewster

   (1) Arkansas
   (2) Colorado
   (3) Massachusetts
   (4) Minnesota
   (5) Montana
   (6) Nevada
   (7) New Jersey
   (8) Texas

ANSWERS TO
SIZES AND SHAPES

1. Oklahoma

2. Michigan

3. Delaware

4. Utah

5. Alaska, Florida, Idaho, Oklahoma, Texas, West Virginia

6. Montana

7. California (San Bernardino County – 20,062 square miles)

8. California (770 miles) and Texas (620 miles)

9. Georgia

10. California

11. Washington

12. Colorado and Wyoming

13. Maryland (near Hancock)

14. Michigan (96,810 square miles)

15. Texas (Kelly Air Force Base – 2,000 x 300 x 90 feet)

16. New York (Verrazano-Narrows Bridge – 4,260 feet)

17. Massachusetts (Boston) and Washington (Seattle) (3,107 miles)

18. New York (Erie Barge Canal – 365 miles)

19. Montana (Fort Peck)

20. Ohio (Cincinnati – 17 tons)

21. California (Oroville Dam)

22. Colorado (Moffat Tunnel – 6.2 miles)

23. Louisiana (Huey P. Long Bridge – 4.4 miles including approach roads)

24. Pennsylvania (Rockville Bridge – 3,810 feet)

25. New Jersey and New York (2.5 miles Lincoln Tunnel)

26. Colorado (Royal Gorge Canyon – 1,053 feet above bed of the Arkansas River)

27.
   a. (7) Texas (Ft. Stockton)
   b. (5) North Dakota (Jamestown)
   c. (3) Minnesota
   d. (1) Colorado
   e. (8) Texas (Houston)
   f. (6) North Dakota (New Salem)
   g. (2) Iowa
   h. (4) Missouri

28. Part I:
   a. (1) Arizona
   b. (2) Illinois
   c. (8) South Dakota
   d. (7) Oregon
   e. (5) North Dakota
   f. (6) Oklahoma
   g. (4) New York
   h. (3) Maine

   Part II:
   a. (4) Minnesota
   b. (2) Colorado
   c. (1) Arkansas
   d. (3) Massachusetts
   e. (6) Nevada
   f. (5) Montana
   g. (7) New Jersey
   h. (8) Texas

SPORTS AND SPOTS

1. The Masters Golf Tournament is held in what state?

2. In what state was basketball invented?

3. What state was the site of the first intercollegiate football game?

4. The largest land-locked swimming pool in the United States is in what state?

5. The origin of ten-pin bowling took place in what state?

6. What state has the smallest city with a National Football League team?

7. In what state was softball invented?

8. In what state did the first triathlon take place?

9. In what state was volleyball invented?

10. Jousting is the official sport of what state?

11. The so-called triple crown of horse races are held in what three states?

12. In what states are the following college football bowls?
   a. Cotton
   b. Fiesta
   c. Orange
   d. Peach
   e. Rose
   f. Sugar

13. In what states are the following auto race tracks and speedways?

   a. Talladega Superspeedway   (1) Alabama
   b. Pan American Speedway   (2) Connecticut (Lakeville)
   c. Lime Rock Park   (3) Florida
   d. Daytona Speedway   (4) Indiana
   e. Beech Ridge Speedway   (5) Maine
   f. Sunset Speedway   (6) Nebraska (Omaha)
   g. Bristol International Raceway   (7) North Carolina (Concord)
   h. Charlotte Motor Speedway   (8) Pennsylvania
   i. Muncie Motor Speedway   (9) Tennessee
   j. Pocono International Raceway   (10) Texas (San Antonio)

14. Match the states to the following golf courses and clubs.

   a. Doral Country Club   (1) California
   b. Bermuda Dunes Country Club   (2) Colorado
   c. St. Andrews   (3) Florida
   d. Southern Hills Country Club   (4) Indiana
   e. Shawnee-on-Delaware   (5) Maryland
   f. Meridian Hills Country Club   (6) New York
   g. Five Farms Course   (7) Oklahoma
   h. Broadmoor Golf Course   (8) Pennsylvania
   i. Ekwanok   (9) Texas
   j. Northwood Country Club   (10) Vermont

15. Match the states to the following ski areas and resorts.

   a. Park City   (1) Arizona
   b. Fairfield Snow Bowl   (2) California
   c. Sun Valley   (3) Colorado
   d. Big Mountain   (4) Idaho
   e. Squaw Valley   (5) Montana
   f. Lake Placid   (6) New York
   g. Woodstock   (7) Oregon
   h. Mount Bachelor   (8) Utah
   i. Crystal Mountain   (9) Vermont
   j. Aspen   (10) Washington

16. In what states are the following horse racing tracks?

   a. Rockingham Park   (1) Arkansas
   b. Gulfstream Park   (2) California
   c. Aqueduct   (3) Florida
   d. Wheeling Downs   (4) Illinois
   e. Pimlico   (5) Kentucky
   f. Santa Anita Park   (6) Maryland
   g. Oaklawn Park   (7) Massachusetts
   h. Hawthorn Race Course   (8) New Hampshire
   i. Suffolk Downs   (9) New Jersey
   j. Churchill Downs   (10) New York
   k. Camden   (11) South Carolina
   l. Garden State   (12) West Virginia

17. In what states are the following sports arenas?

    a. Cow Palace
    b. Cobo Arena
    c. Freedom Hall
    d. Hara Arena
    e. Kiel Auditorium
    f. Madison Square Garden
    g. Spectrum
    h. Tingley Coliseum
    i. Omni Coliseum
    j. Kingdome

    (1) California (San Francisco)
    (2) Georgia (Atlanta)
    (3) Kentucky (Louisville)
    (4) Michigan (Detroit)
    (5) Missouri (St. Louis)
    (6) New Mexico (Albuquerque)
    (7) New York (New York City)
    (8) Ohio (Dayton)
    (9) Pennsylvania (Philadelphia)
    (10) Washington (Seattle)

18. In what states are the following sports stadiums?

    a. Riverfront
    b. Shea
    c. Candlestick Park
    d. Fenway Park
    e. Soldier Field
    f. Busch Memorial
    g. Three-Rivers
    h. Metropolitan
    i. Arlington Stadium
    j. Mile High Stadium

    (1) California (San Francisco)
    (2) Colorado (Denver)
    (3) Illinois (Chicago)
    (4) Massachusetts (Boston)
    (5) Minnesota (Bloomington)
    (6) Missouri (St. Louis)
    (7) New York (New York City)
    (8) Ohio (Cincinnati)
    (9) Pennsylvania (Pittsburgh)
    (10) Texas

19. In what states are the following halls of fame?

    a. Hall of Fame of the Trotter
    b. Greyhound Hall of Fame
    c. National Rodeo Hall of Fame
    d. National Professional Football Hall of Fame
    e. United States Ski Hall of Fame
    f. National Basketball Hall of Fame
    g. International Swimming Hall of Fame
    h. International Tennis Hall of Fame
    i. National Bowling Hall of Fame
    j. National Track and Field Hall of Fame

    (1) Florida (Ft. Lauderdale)
    (2) Kansas (Abilene)
    (3) Massachusetts (Springfield)
    (4) Michigan (Ishpeming)
    (5) New York (Goshen)
    (6) Ohio (Canton)
    (7) Oklahoma (Oklahoma City)
    (8) Rhode Island (Newport)
    (9) West Virginia (Charleston)
    (10) Wisconsin (Greendale)

ANSWERS TO
SPORTS AND SPOTS

1. Georgia (Augusta)

2. Massachusetts (Springfield)

3. New Jersey (Princeton and Rutgers)

4. Ohio (Willow Lake in Warren – 600 x 150 feet)

5. Connecticut (1845)

6. Wisconsin (Green Bay)

7. Illinois (Chicago in 1887 by George Hancock)

8. Hawaii (1978)

9. Massachusetts (Holyoke)

10. Maryland

11. Kentucky (Derby), Maryland (Preakness), New York (Belmont)

12. Texas, Arizona, Florida, Georgia, California, Louisiana

13. a. (1) Alabama
    b. (10) Texas
    c. (2) Connecticut
    d. (3) Florida
    e. (5) Maine
    f. (6) Nebraska
    g. (9) Tennessee
    h. (7) North Carolina
    i. (4) Indiana
    j. (8) Pennsylvania

14. a. (3) Florida
    b. (1) California
    c. (6) New York
    d. (7) Oklahoma
    e. (8) Pennsylvania
    f. (4) Indiana
    g. (5) Maryland
    h. (2) Colorado
    i. (10) Vermont
    j. (9) Texas

15. a. (8) Utah
    b. (1) Arizona
    c. (4) Idaho
    d. (5) Montana
    e. (2) California
    f. (6) New York
    g. (9) Vermont
    h. (7) Oregon
    i. (10) Washington
    j. (3) Colorado

16. a. (8) New Hampshire
    b. (3) Florida
    c. (10) New York
    d. (12) West Virginia
    e. (6) Maryland
    f. (2) California
    g. (1) Arkansas
    h. (4) Illinois
    i. (7) Massachusetts
    j. (5) Kentucky
    k. (11) South Carolina
    l. (9) New Jersey

17. a. (1) California
    b. (4) Michigan
    c. (3) Kentucky
    d. (8) Ohio
    e. (5) Missouri
    f. (7) New York
    g. (9) Pennsylvania
    h. (6) New Mexico
    i. (2) Georgia
    j. (10) Washington

18. a. (8) Ohio
    b. (7) New York
    c. (1) California
    d. (4) Massachusetts
    e. (3) Illinois
    f. (6) Missouri
    g. (9) Pennsylvania
    h. (5) Minnesota
    i. (10) Texas
    j. (2) Colorado

19. a. (5) New York
    b. (2) Kansas
    c. (7) Oklahoma
    d. (6) Ohio
    e. (4) Michigan
    f. (3) Massachusetts
    g. (1) Florida
    h. (8) Rhode Island
    i. (10) Wisconsin
    j. (9) West Virginia

GENERAL INDEX

ORDER FORM

HiStory ink Books
P.O. Box 52
Hat Creek, CA 96040

<u>Quantity</u>	<u>Title (all books paperback)</u>
_____	*Stories of the Klamath National Forest—The First 50 Years: 1905 – 1955* ($16.95)
_____	*Memories From the Land of Siskiyou: Past Lives and Times in Siskiyou County* ($19.95)
_____	*Fort Jones (CA) 1852 – 1858: Military Notes* ($22.00)
_____	*A World War II Diary by Lawrence E. Davies, The West Coast Correspondent for The New York Times* ($12.95)
_____	*Photographic Images of the Klamath National Forest in Siskiyou and Humboldt Counties: A Historical Journey* (plus surprise bonus book) ($20.00)
_____	*Historical And Commemorative Signs, Plaques and Monuments in Siskiyou County, California* ($14.95)
_____	*State the State: More Than 2,500 Questions and Answers from Alabama to Wyoming* ($10.00)
_____	*Thirty Country Road Loop Trips in Northern California: All North of Sacramento* (available soon – request notification)
_____	Do <u>not</u> ship any books at this time – send informational brochures on _____ (free) (name of book or books)

I enclose $_____ (including 7.25% sales tax for California residents and $2.00 shipping for each book)

Name _____

Address _____

City or Town _____ State _____ Zip _____

Payment may be made by personal check, cashier's check or money order. Check should be made payable to: **HiStory ink Books**.

Cut Along Line